THE YALE SHAKESPEARE

Revised Edition

General Editors

Helge Kökeritz and Charles T. Prouty

Published on the fund

given to the Yale University Press in 1917

by the members of the

Kingsley Trust Association

(Scroll and Key Society of Yale College)

to commemorate the seventy-fifth anniversary

of the founding of the society

THE YALE SHAKESPEARE

THE TRAGEDY OF ROMEO

AND JULIET

Edited by Richard Hosley

LUX ET VERITAS

NEW HAVEN: YALE UNIVERSITY PRESS

London: Geoffrey Cumberlege, Oxford University Press

Preface of the General Editors

AS the late Professor Tucker Brooke has observed, practically all modern editions of Shakespeare are 18th-century versions of the plays, based on the additions, alterations, and emendations of editors of that period. It has been our purpose, as it was Professor Brooke's, to give the modern reader Shakespeare's plays in the approximate form of their original appearance.

About half the plays appeared in quarto form before the publication of the First Folio in 1623. Thus for a large number of plays the only available text is that of the Folio. In the case of quarto plays our policy has been to use that text as the basis of the edition, unless it is clear that the text has been contaminated.

Interesting for us today is the fact that there are no act or scene divisions in the Quartos with the exception of *Othello*, which does mark Acts I, II, IV, and V but lacks indications of scenes. Even in the Folio, although act divisions are generally noted, only a part of the scenes are divided. In no case, either in Quarto or Folio, is there any indication of the place of action. The manifold scene divisions for the battle in such a play as *Antony and Cleopatra*, together with such locations as "Another part of the field," are the additions of the 18th century.

We have eliminated all indications of the place and time of action, because there is no authority for them in the originals and because Shakespeare gives such information, when it is requisite for understanding the play, through the dialogue of the actors. We have been sparing in our use of added scene and, in some cases, act divisions, because these frequently impede the flow of the action, which in Shakespeare's time was curiously like that of modern films.

Spelling has been modernized except when the original clearly indicates a pronunciation unlike our own, e.g. *desart* (desert), *divel* (devil), *banket* (banquet), and often in such Elizabethan syncopations as *stolne* (stol'n), and *tane* (ta'en). In reproducing such forms we have followed the inconsistent usage of the original.

We have also preserved the original capitalization when this is a part of the meaning. In like manner we have tended to adopt the lineation of the original in many cases where modern editors print prose as verse or verse as prose. We have, moreover, followed the original punctuation wherever it was practicable.

In verse we print a final *-ed* to indicate its full syllabic value, otherwise *'d*. In prose we have followed the inconsistencies of the original in this respect.

Our general practice has been to include in footnotes all information a reader needs for immediate understanding of the given page. In somewhat empiric fashion we repeat glosses as we think the reader needs to be reminded of the meaning. Further information is given in notes (indicated by the letter *N* in the footnotes) to be found at the back of each volume. Appendices deal with the text and sources of the play.

Square brackets indicate material not found in the original text. Long emendations or lines taken from another authoritative text of a play are indicated in the footnotes for the information of the reader. We have silently corrected obvious typographical errors.

CONTENTS

[THE ACTORS' NAMES

ESCALUS, *Prince of Verona*
PARIS, *a young nobleman, kinsman to the Prince*
MONTAGUE
CAPULET } *heads of two opposed Houses*
2. CAPULET, *cousin to Capulet*
ROMEO, *son to Montague*
MERCUTIO, *kinsman to the Prince*
BENVOLIO, *nephew to Montague* } *friends to Romeo*
TYBALT, *nephew to Capulet's Wife*
FRIAR LAWRENCE
FRIAR JOHN } *Franciscans*
BALTHASAR, *servant to Romeo*
ABRAM, *servant to Montague*
SAMPSON
GREGORY } *servants to Capulet*
PETER, *servant to Juliet's Nurse*
AN APOTHECARY
THREE MUSICIANS
PAGE TO PARIS
CHIEF WATCHMAN
CHORUS

MONTAGUE'S WIFE
CAPULET'S WIFE
JULIET, *daughter to Capulet*
NURSE TO JULIET

*Citizens of Verona, Kinsfolk of both Houses, Maskers,
     Servingmen, Pages, Watchmen, and the Prince's
     Train*]

THE MOST EXCELLENT AND LAMENTABLE TRAGEDY OF ROMEO AND JULIET

The Prologue

[*Enter Chorus.*]

CHORUS. *Two households both alike in dignity*
(In fair Verona where we lay our scene)
From ancient grudge break to new mutiny,
Where civil blood makes civil hands unclean.
From forth the fatal loins of these two foes   5
A pair of star-cross'd lovers take their life,
Whose misadventur'd piteous overthrows
Doth with their death bury their parents' strife.
The fearful passage of their death-mark'd love
And the continuance of their parents' rage   10
(Which but their children's end nought could re-
  move)
Is now the two hours' traffic of our stage,
The which if you with patient ears attend
What here shall miss our toil shall strive to mend.
          [*Exit.*]

The Prologue N. (N refers throughout to the corresponding note given at the end of the text.) 1 **dignity** rank. 3 **mutiny** strife. 4 **civil** of citizens. 6 **star-cross'd** predestined to be thwarted. 9 **passage** course. 12 **two hours** N. 14 **miss** be lacking.

[*Act I*

SCENE 1]

Enter Sampson and Gregory with swords and bucklers, of the House of Capulet.

Sampson. Gregory, on my word we 'll not carry coals.

Gregory. No, for then we should be colliers.

Sampson. I mean, and we be in choler we 'll draw.

Gregory. Ay, while you live draw your neck out of collar. ⁶

Sampson. I strike quickly, being moved.

Gregory. But thou art not quickly moved to strike.

Sampson. A dog of the house of Montague moves me. ¹⁰

Gregory. To move is to stir, and to be valiant is to stand. Therefore if thou art moved thou run'st away.

Sampson. A dog of that house shall move me to stand. I will take the wall of any man or maid of Montague's. ¹⁶

Gregory. That shows thee a weak slave, for the weakest goes to the wall.

Sampson. 'Tis true, and therefore women, being the weaker vessels, are ever thrust to the wall. Therefore

---

Act I, Scene 1 N. 1 **carry coals** i.e. do dirty work, be imposed upon. 1–11 **coals . . . move** N. 3 **colliers** coal-dealers. 4 **and if.** **choler** that one of the four humors which produces anger. 15 **take the wall** N. 18 **goes to the wall** i.e. is thrust out of the way (proverbial). 20 **weaker vessels** see 1 Peter 3:7.

3

I will push Montague's men from the wall and thrust his maids to the wall.

Gregory. The quarrel is between our masters and us their men.   24

Sampson. 'Tis all one, I will show myself a tyrant. When I have fought with the men I will be civil with the maids—I will cut off their heads.

Gregory. The heads of the maids?

Sampson. Ay, the heads of the maids or their maidenheads. Take it in what sense thou wilt.   30

Gregory. They must take it in sense that feel it.

Sampson. Me they shall feel while I am able to stand, and 'tis known I am a pretty piece of flesh.

Gregory. 'Tis well thou art not fish—if thou hadst, thou hadst been poor-john. Draw thy tool! Here comes two of the house of Montagues.   36

Enter two Servingmen ⟨of the Montagues⟩.

Sampson. My naked weapon is out. Quarrel, I will back thee.

Gregory. How? turn thy back and run?

Sampson. Fear me not.   40

Gregory. No marry, I fear thee!

Sampson. Let us take the law of our sides—let them begin.

Gregory. I will frown as I pass by, and let them take it as they list.   45

24 **men** servants. 26 **civil** orderly, well-governed (quibble on 'polite'). 31 **in** Q1; Q2 omits. **sense** physical sensation. 35 **poor-john** dried salt cod. 36 **two** Q1; Q2 omits. SD **two** So Q1; Q2 *two other.* (SD is used throughout to indicate stage direction.) ⟨**of the Montagues**⟩ (Throughout the text stage directions and lines from Q1 are enclosed in angle brackets.) 38 **back** support (but Gregory quibbles). 40 **Fear me not** don't worry about me (Gregory quibbles). 41 **marry** indeed (by the Virgin Mary). 45 **list** please.

4

Sampson. Nay, as they dare. I will bite my thumb at them, which is disgrace to them if they bear it.

Abram. Do you bite your thumb at us, sir?

Sampson. I do bite my thumb, sir.

Abram. Do you bite your thumb at us, sir?   50

Sampson. Is the law of our side if I say 'ay'?

Gregory. No.

Sampson. No sir, I do not bite my thumb at you, sir. But I bite my thumb, sir.

Gregory. Do you quarrel, sir?   55

Abram. Quarrel, sir? No sir.

Sampson. But if you do, sir, I am for you. I serve as good a man as you.

Abram. No better.

Sampson. Well, sir.   60

Enter Benvolio.

Gregory. Say 'better,' here comes one of my master's kinsmen.

Sampson. Yes, better, sir.

Abram. You lie.   64

Sampson. Draw, if you be men. Gregory, remember thy washing blow.   *They fight.*

Benvolio. Part, fools!

Put up your swords, you know not what you do.

Enter Tybalt.

Tybalt. What! art thou drawn among these heartless hinds?

46 **bite my thumb** an insult N. 48 **Abram** one of the Montague Servingmen. SD Benvolio N. 61 **one** Tybalt, whom Gregory sees approaching. 63–83 **Yes, better, sir . . . seek a foe** N. 66 **washing** swashing, swashbuckling. **washing blow** i.e. of sword against buckler (see II.3.28 N). 69 **heartless** cowardly (pun on 'hart,' stag). **hinds** menials (quibble on 'female deer').

5

Turn thee, Benvolio, look upon thy death.   70

Benvolio. I do but keep the peace—put up thy
 sword
Or manage it to part these men with me.

Tybalt. What! drawn and talk of peace? I hate the
 word,
As I hate hell, all Montagues and thee.   74
Have at thee, coward.   [*They fight.*]

Enter three or four Citizens with clubs or partisans.

Citizens. Clubs, bills and partisans! Strike! Beat
 them down!
Down with the Capulets! Down with the Montagues!

Enter old Capulet in his gown, and his Wife.

Capulet. What noise is this? give me my long sword,
 ho!

Wife. A crutch, a crutch! why call you for a sword?

Enter old Montague and his Wife.

Capulet. My sword, I say, old Montague is come
And flourishes his blade in spite of me.   81

Montague. Thou villain Capulet! Hold me not, let
 me go.

Montague's Wife. Thou shalt not stir one foot to
 seek a foe.

Enter Prince Escalus with his Train.

Prince. Rebellious subjects, enemies to peace,
Profaners of this neighbor-stained steel—   85

71 put up sheathe. SD **partisans** broad-bladed pikes. 76 **Citizens**
Q2 *Offi.* N. Clubs . . . **partisans** a rallying cry of London ap-
prentices. **bills** ax-headed spears. SD **gown** dressing gown. 78 **long
sword** N. SD **Enter old Montague . . . Wife** N. 81 **spite** defiance. 85 **neighbor-stained** stained with neighbors' blood.

6

Will they not hear? What ho! you men, you beasts,
That quench the fire of your pernicious rage
With purple fountains issuing from your veins—
On pain of torture, from those bloody hands
Throw your mistemper'd weapons to the ground   90
And hear the sentence of your moved Prince.
Three civil brawls, bred of an airy word,
By thee, old Capulet and Montague,
Have thrice disturb'd the quiet of our streets
And made Verona's ancient citizens   95
Cast by their grave beseeming ornaments
To wield old partisans, in hands as old,
Canker'd with peace, to part your canker'd hate.
If ever you disturb our streets again
Your lives shall pay the forfeit of the peace.   100
For this time all the rest depart away.
You Capulet, shall go along with me.
And Montague, come you this afternoon
To know our farther pleasure in this case
To old Freetown, our common judgment place.   105
Once more, on pain of death, all men depart.
Exeunt [all but Montague, his Wife and Benvolio].
  Montague. Who set this ancient quarrel new
      abroach?
Speak nephew, were you by when it began?
  Benvolio. Here were the servants of your adversary
And yours, close fighting ere I did approach.   110
I drew to part them. In the instant came

90 mistemper'd tempered for evil (quibble on 'ill-tempered'). 91
sentence decree. moved angered. 92 airy light, trifling. 98
Canker'd . . . canker'd corroded . . . malignant. 99–100 If ever
you disturb . . . the peace N. 100 forfeit penalty for the breach.
105 Freetown Brooke's translation of the Italian *Villa Franca*.
107 new again. abroach broached and left running (like beer from
a cask); compare I.4.198 N.

7

The fiery Tybalt with his sword prepar'd,
Which as he breath'd defiance to my ears
He swung about his head and cut the winds,
Who, nothing hurt withal, hiss'd him in scorn.   115
While we were interchanging thrusts and blows,
Came more and more, and fought on part and part
Till the Prince came, who parted either part.

   Montague's Wife. O where is Romeo? saw you him
    today?
Right glad I am he was not at this fray.   120

   Benvolio. Madam, an hour before the worship'd Sun
Peer'd forth the golden window of the East,
A troubled mind drove me to walk abroad,
Where underneath the grove of sycamore
That westward rooteth from this city side,   125
So early walking did I see your son.
Towards him I made, but he was ware of me
And stole into the covert of the wood.
I, measuring his affections by my own,
(Which then most sought where most might not be
    found,   130
Being one too many by my weary self)
Pursu'd my humor, not pursuing his,
And gladly shunn'd who gladly fled from me.

   Montague. Many a morning hath he there been
    seen,
With tears augmenting the fresh morning's dew,   135
Adding to clouds more clouds with his deep sighs;
But all so soon as the all-cheering Sun
Should in the farthest East begin to draw

---

115 **withal** thereby. 117 **part and part** either side. 118 **either part**
both parties. 123 **drove** Q2 *drive* **abroad** away from home. 129
affections feelings. 130 **where** a place where. **most** most people.
132 **humor** inclination (for solitude). 133 **who** him who. 134–45
Many a morning . . . remove N.

8

The shady curtains from Aurora's bed,
Away from light steals home my heavy son   140
And private in his chamber pens himself,
Shuts up his windows, locks fair daylight out
And makes himself an artificial night.
Black and portentous must this humor prove
Unless good counsel may the cause remove.   145
  Benvolio. My noble uncle, do you know the cause?
  Montague. I neither know it nor can learn of him.
  Benvolio. Have you importun'd him by any means?
  Montague. Both by myself and many other friends.
But he, his own affections' counselor,   150
Is to himself—I will not say how true—
But to himself so secret and so close,
So far from sounding and discovery,
As is the bud bit with an envious worm
Ere he can spread his sweet leaves to the air   155
Or dedicate his beauty to the sun.
Could we but learn from whence his sorrows grow,
We would as willingly give cure as know.

Enter Romeo.

  Benvolio. See where he comes. So please you, step
    aside,
I'll know his grievance or be much denied.   160
  Montague. I would thou wert so happy by thy stay
To hear true shrift. Come madam, let's away.
              Exeunt [*Montague and his Wife*].
  Benvolio. Good morrow, cousin.

139 **Aurora** goddess of the dawn. 140 **heavy** melancholy. 148 **importun'd** questioned insistently (stressed – ⌣ –). 150 **his . . . counselor** who keeps his own feelings secret. 152 **so secret and so close** N. **close** reticent. 153 **sounding** fathoming. 154 **envious** malicious. 156 **sun** Q2 *same*. 161 **happy** fortunate. 162 **shrift** confession. 163 **Good morrow** good morning.

Romeo.   Is the day so young?

Benvolio. But new struck nine.

Romeo.   Ay me, sad hours seem long.
Was that my father that went hence so fast?   165

Benvolio. It was. What sadness lengthens Romeo's
   hours?

Romeo. Not having that which, having, makes them
   short.

Benvolio. In love!

Romeo. Out—

Benvolio. Of love?   170

Romeo. Out of her favor where I am in love.

Benvolio. Alas that Love, so gentle in his view,
Should be so tyrannous and rough in proof.

Romeo. Alas that Love, whose view is muffled still,
Should without eyes see pathways to his will.   175
Where shall we dine?—O me! what fray was here?
Yet tell me not, for I have heard it all,
Here 's much to do with hate but more with love.
Why then, O brawling love, O loving hate,
O anything of nothing first created,   180
O heavy lightness, serious vanity,
Misshapen Chaos of well-seeming forms,
Feather of lead, bright smoke, cold fire, sick health,
Still-waking sleep that is not what it is—
This love feel I that feel no love in this.   185
Dost thou not laugh?

Benvolio.   No coz, I rather weep.

Romeo. Good heart, at what?

Benvolio.   At thy good heart's oppression.

---

164 **new** recently. 167 **having, makes** if I had it, would make.
172 **Love** Cupid. **view** appearance. 173 **proof** experience. 174 **view**
sight. **muffled** blindfolded. **still** always. 175 **his will** i.e. to make
us fall in love. 179–84 **brawling love . . . sleep** N. 182 **seeming**
Q1; Q2 *seeing*. 184 **Still-waking** ever-wakeful. 186 **coz** cousin.

Romeo. Why, such is love's transgression.
Griefs of mine own lie heavy in my breast,
Which thou wilt propagate to have it press'd   190
With more of thine. This love that thou hast shown
Doth add more grief to too much of mine own.
Love is a smoke made with the fume of sighs,
Being purg'd a fire sparkling in lovers' eyes,
Being vex'd a sea nourish'd with loving tears.   195
What is it else? a madness most discreet,
A choking gall and a preserving sweet.
Farewell, my coz.
    Benvolio.   Soft, I will go along,
And if you leave me so you do me wrong.
    Romeo. Tut, I have left myself, I am not here,   200
This is not Romeo, he's some other where.
    Benvolio. Tell me in sadness, who is that you love?
    Romeo. What! shall I groan and tell thee?
    Benvolio. Groan? why no, but sadly tell me who.
    Romeo. Bid a sick man in sadness make his will—
Ah, word ill urg'd to one that is so ill.   206
In sadness, cousin, I do love a woman.
    Benvolio. I aim'd so near when I suppos'd you lov'd.
    Romeo. A right good markman! and she's fair I
        love.   209
    Benvolio. A right fair mark, fair coz, is soonest hit.
    Romeo. Well, in that hit you miss. She'll not be hit
With Cupid's arrow. She hath Dian's wit,
And in strong proof of chastity well arm'd

190 **propagate** multiply. 194 **Being purg'd** when the smoke has
cleared away. 198 **Soft** wait a moment. 199 **And if** if. 200 **left** Q2
lost N. 202 **sadness** seriousness (Romeo quibbles on 'sorrow').
that she whom. 204 **sadly** seriously. 205 **Bid a . . . make** Q1; Q2
A . . . makes. 206 **ill urg'd** inopportunely mentioned. 211 **in
. . . you miss** i.e. right in general but not in this case. 212 **Dian's
wit** the goddess Diana's wisdom to remain a virgin. 213 **proof**
armor.

11

From Love's weak childish bow she lives uncharm'd.
She will not stay the siege of loving terms,   215
Nor bide th' encounter of assailing eyes,
Nor ope her lap to saint-seducing gold.
O she is rich in beauty, only poor
That when she dies, with beauty dies her store.
  Benvolio. Then she hath sworn that she will still
     live chaste?   220
  Romeo. She hath, and in that sparing makes huge
     waste,
For Beauty, starv'd with her severity,
Cuts beauty off from all posterity.
She is too fair, too wise, wisely too fair,
To merit bliss by making me despair.   225
She hath forsworn to love, and in that vow
Do I live dead that live to tell it now.
  Benvolio. Be rul'd by me, forget to think of her.
  Romeo. O teach me how I should forget to think.
  Benvolio. By giving liberty unto thine eyes,   230
Examine other beauties.
  Romeo.   'Tis the way
To call hers, exquisite, in question more.
These happy masks that kiss fair ladies' brows,
Being black, puts us in mind they hide the fair.
He that is strucken blind cannot forget   235
The precious treasure of his eyesight lost.
Show me a mistress that is passing fair—
What doth her beauty serve but as a note
Where I may read who pass'd that passing fair?

214 From by. 215 stay endure. 218–19 rich . . . store N. 222
starv'd with killed by. 225 merit . . . despair i.e. earn salvation
through chastity. 226 forsworn sworn not. 232 call . . . in question
contemplate. 237 passing surpassingly. 238–9 note . . . fair
reminder of a fairer mistress.

12

Farewell, thou canst not teach me to forget.   240
  Benvolio. I'll pay that doctrine or else die in debt.
                                    Exeunt.

[SCENE 2]

Enter Capulet, County Paris and the Clown.

  Capulet. But Montague is bound as well as I
In penalty alike, and 'tis not hard, I think,
For men so old as we to keep the peace.
  Paris. Of honorable reck'ning are you both,
And pity 'tis you liv'd at odds so long.   5
But now, my lord, what say you to my suit?
  Capulet. But saying o'er what I have said before—
My child is yet a stranger in the world,
She hath not seen the change of fourteen years.
Let two more summers wither in their pride   10
Ere we may think her ripe to be a bride.
  Paris. Younger than she are happy mothers made.
  Capulet. And too soon marr'd are those so early
          made.
Earth hath swallow'd all my hopes but she—
She 's the hopeful lady of my earth.   15
But woo her, gentle Paris, get her heart,
My will to her consent is but a part.
And she agreed, within her scope of choice
Lies my consent and fair according voice.

241 **pay . . . debt** give that instruction despite the cost. SD
County count. **Clown** countryman, peasant (Capulet's servant).
1 **bound** bonded (to keep the peace). 4 **reck'ning** reputation. 9
fourteen years see I.3.12 N. 13 **marr'd . . . made** N. 14 **Earth
. . . she** i.e. my other children are buried. 15 **earth** body (since
she will perpetuate his line). 19 **according** consenting.

This night I hold an old accustom'd feast,   20
Whereto I have invited many a guest
Such as I love, and you among the store
One more, most welcome, makes my number more.
At my poor house look to behold this night   24
Earth-treading stars that make dark heaven light.
Such comfort as do lusty young men feel
When well-apparel'd April on the heel
Of limping Winter treads, e'en such delight
Among fresh fennel buds shall you this night
Inherit at my house—hear all, all see,   30
And like her most whose merit most shall be;
Which, on more view of many, mine (being one)
May stand in number though in reck'ning none.
Come, go with me. Go sirrah, trudge about
Through fair Verona. Find those persons out   35
Whose names are written there, and to them say
My house and welcome on their pleasure stay.

                            Exeunt [*Capulet and Paris*].

   Servant. Find them out whose names are written?
Here it is written that the shoemaker should meddle
with his yard and the tailor with his last, the fisher
with his pencil and the painter with his nets. But I
am sent to find those persons whose names are here
writ, and can never find what names the writing per-

20 feast the rhyme indicates the common Elizabethan pronunciation 'fest.' 22 store gathering. 26 lusty vigorous. 28 e'en Q2
euen (silently emended throughout). 29 fennel a bridal flower
(supposedly an aphrodisiac). 30 Inherit possess. 32 Which with
whom (referring to 'her'). on Q2 *one*. mine my daughter. 33 none
quibble on 'One is no number' (proverbial; compare Sonnet 136).
34 sirrah term of address to an inferior (the servant). 39–41 shoemaker . . . nets N. 39 meddle busy himself. 40 yard measuring
rod. 41 pencil brush.

son hath here writ. I must to the learned. In good
time!   45

Enter Benvolio and Romeo.

Benvolio. Tut man, one fire burns out another's
    burning,
One pain is lessen'd by another's anguish;
Turn giddy and be holp by backward turning,
One desp'rate grief cures with another's languish.
Take thou some new infection to thy eye   50
And the rank poison of the old will die.
Romeo. Your plantain leaf is excellent for that.
Benvolio. For what, I pray thee?
Romeo.   For your broken shin.
Benvolio. Why Romeo, art thou mad?
Romeo. Not mad, but bound more than a madman
    is,   55
Shut up in prison, kept without my food,
Whipp'd and tormented, and—Godden, good fellow.
Servant. Godgigoden. I pray sir, can you read?
Romeo. Ay, mine own fortune in my misery.   59
Servant. Perhaps you have learn'd it without book.
But I pray, can you read anything you see?
Romeo. Ay, if I know the letters and the language.
Servant. Ye say honestly, rest you merry!
Romeo. Stay fellow, I can read.

He reads the letter.

44 **in good time** in the nick of time. 48 **holp** helped. 49 **languish**
suffering. 52 **plantain leaf** medication N. 53 **broken** with the skin
broken. 55–7 **bound . . . tormented** N. 57 **Godden** good e'en
(good evening, used after noon). 58 **Godgigoden** God give ye good
e'en. 60 **without book** by heart. 63 **rest you merry** God keep you
merry. SD **letter** document.

> *Signior Martino and his wife and daughters,* 65
> *County Anselm and his beauteous sisters,*
> *The lady widow of Vitruvio,*
> *Signior Placentio and his lovely nieces,*
> *Mercutio and his brother Valentine,*
> *Mine uncle Capulet, his wife and daughters,* 70
> *My fair niece Rosaline and Livia,*
> *Signior Valentio and his cousin Tybalt,*
> *Lucio and the lively Helena.*

A fair assembly, whither should they come?
Servant. Up— 75
Romeo. Whither? to supper?
Servant. To our house.
Romeo. Whose house?
Servant. My master's. 79
Romeo. Indeed I should have ask'd thee that before.
Servant. Now I 'll tell you without asking. My master is the great rich Capulet, and if you be not of the house of Montagues, I pray come and crush a cup of wine. Rest you merry! [*Exit.*]
Benvolio. At this same ancient feast of Capulet's
Sups the fair Rosaline, whom thou so loves, 86
With all th' admired beauties of Verona.
Go thither and with unattainted eye
Compare her face with some that I shall show,
And I will make thee think thy swan a crow. 90
Romeo. When the devout religion of mine eye
Maintains such falsehood, then turn tears to fires,

65–73 Signior Martino . . . Helena prose in Q1–2. 67 Vitruvio
Q1–2 *Vtruuio*. 71 and Q1; Q2 omits N. 76 to supper N. 80 thee
Q1; Q2 *you*; see I.2.71 N. 83. crush finish off, drink down N.
85 ancient i.e. 'old accustom'd' (I.2.20). 88 unattainted unin-
fected, unprejudiced. 91–4 devout religion . . . heretics N.

16

And these who, often drown'd, could never die,
Transparent heretics, be burnt for liars.
One fairer than my love? th' all-seeing Sun   95
Ne'er saw her match since first the world begun.

Benvolio. Tut, you saw her fair none else being by,
Herself pois'd with herself in either eye.
But in that crystal scales let there be weigh'd
Your lady's love against some other maid   100
That I will show you shining at this feast,
And she shall scant show well that now seems best.

Romeo. I 'll go along, no such sight to be shown,
But to rejoice in splendor of mine own.   [*Exeunt.*]

[SCENE 3]

Enter Capulet's Wife and Nurse.

Wife. Nurse, where 's my daughter? call her forth
to me.

Nurse. Now by my maidenhead at twelve year old, I
bade her come. What! lamb, what! ladybird. God
forbid, where 's this girl? What! Juliet.   5

Enter Juliet.

Juliet. How now, who calls?

Nurse. Your mother.

Juliet. Madam, I am here, what is your will?   8

Wife. This is the matter. Nurse, give leave awhile,
we must talk in secret. Nurse, come back again, I

93 **these** i.e. my eyes. 94 **Transparent** bright (quibble on 'easily
detected'). 98 **pois'd** weighed. 100 **lady's love** i.e. lady-love. 102
scant scarcely. 3–5 **Now . . . Juliet** N. 4 **ladybird** sweetheart
(literally, a small beetle). SD **Juliet** N. 9 **matter** business. **give
leave** leave us.

have remember'd me, thou's hear our counsel. Thou knowest my daughter 's of a pretty age?

Nurse. Faith, I can tell her age unto an hour.

Wife. She 's not fourteen. 14

Nurse. I'll lay fourteen of my teeth (and yet to my teen be it spoken, I have but four) she 's not fourteen. How long is it now to Lammas-tide?

Wife. A fortnight and odd days. 18

Nurse. Even or odd, of all days in the year, come Lammas Eve at night shall she be fourteen. Susan and she (God rest all Christian souls) were of an age. Well, Susan is with God, she was too good for me. But as I said, on Lammas Eve at night shall she be fourteen, that shall she, marry, I remember it well. 'Tis since the earthquake now eleven years, and she was wean'd (I never shall forget it) of all the days of the year upon that day, for I had then laid wormwood to my dug, sitting in the sun under the dovehouse wall. My lord and you were then at Mantua —nay, I do bear a brain. But as I said, when it did taste the wormwood on the nipple of my dug and felt it bitter (pretty fool! to see it tetchy and fall out with the dug), 'Shake!' quoth the dovehouse; 'twas no need, I trow, to bid me trudge. And since that time it is eleven years, for then she could stand high-lone. Nay, by th' rood, she could have run and waddled all about, for even the day before she broke her brow, and then my husband (God be with his

11 **thou's** thou shalt. **counsel** secret consultation. 12 **a pretty age** N. 13 **an** so Q2; Q1 *a.* 15 **lay** wager 16 **teen** sorrow. 17 **Lammas-tide** Lammas-time (August 1) N. 25 **since . . . eleven years** N. 30 **bear a brain** keep my memory. 32 **tetchy** fretful. 32 **fall out** quarrel. 33 **the dug** so Q2; Q1 *Dugge.* **'Shake!'** N. 34 **I trow** I assure you. 36 **high-lone** quite alone. **rood** cross. 37 **broke** broke the skin of.

soul, 'a was a merry man) took up the child. 'Yea,'
quoth he, 'dost thou fall upon thy face? Thou wilt
fall backward when thou hast more wit, wilt thou
not, Jule?' And by my holidam, the pretty wretch
left crying and said 'Ay.' To see now how a jest
shall come about! I warrant and I should live a thousand years I never should forget it. 'Wilt thou not,
Jule?' quoth he, and pretty fool, it stinted and said
'Ay.'   47

Wife. Enough of this, I pray thee hold thy peace.

Nurse. Yes madam. Yet I cannot choose but laugh
—to think it should leave crying and say 'Ay.' And
yet I warrant it had upon it brow a bump as big as
a young cock'rel's stone (a perilous knock) and it
cried bitterly. 'Yea,' quoth my husband, 'fall'st upon
thy face? Thou wilt fall backward when thou comest
to age, wilt thou not, Jule?' It stinted and said 'Ay.'

Juliet. And stint thou too, I pray thee, Nurse,
say I.   57

Nurse. Peace, I have done. God mark thee to his
grace, thou wast the prettiest babe that e'er I nurs'd.
And I might live to see thee married once, I have my
wish.

Wife. Marry, that 'marry' is the very theme
I came to talk of. Tell me, daughter Juliet,
How stands your dispositions to be marry'd?

Juliet. It is an honor that I dream not of.   65

Nurse. An honor! were not I thine only nurse I
would say thou hadst suck'd wisdom from thy teat.

39 **'a** he. 41 **wit** sense. 42 **by my holidam** a mild oath N. 44 **come
about** come true. 46 **stinted** stopped. 51 **it brow** its brow. 52 **stone**
testicle. 58 **mark** elect. 60 **once** some day. 64 **How . . . to be** how
are you disposed toward being. 65, 66 **honor** Q1; Q2 *houre.* 67 **thy**
i.e. the Nurse's.

Wife. Well, think of marriage now. Younger than
    you
Here in Verona, ladies of esteem,
Are made already mothers. By my count,   70
I was your mother much upon these years
That you are now a maid. Thus then in brief,
The valiant Paris seeks you for his love.
  Nurse. A man, young lady, lady, such a man as all
the world. Why, he 's a man of wax.   75
  Wife. Verona's summer hath not such a flower.
  Nurse. Nay he 's a flower, in faith a very flower.
  Wife. What say you, can you love the gentleman?
This night you shall behold him at our feast,
Read o'er the volume of young Paris' face   80
And find delight writ there with Beauty's pen,
Examine every married lineament
And see how one another lends content,
And what obscur'd in this fair volume lies
Find written in the margent of his eyes.   85
This precious book of love, this unbound lover,
To beautify him only lacks a cover.
The fish lives in the sea, and 'tis much pride
For fair-without the fair-within to hide.
That book in many's eyes doth share the glory   90
That in gold clasps locks in the golden story.
So shall you share all that he doth possess,
By having him making yourself no less.
  Nurse. No less! nay, bigger! women grow by men.

71–2 **I was your mother . . . maid** N. 75 **of wax** perfectly beautiful (like a wax figure). 79 **This night . . . feast** N. 82 **marry'd**
harmonious. 83 **content** a pleasing impression. 85 **margent** margin
(where explanatory notes were written). 86 **unbound** without
binding (quibble on 'unattached'). 87 **cover** binding (quibble on
'wife'). 88 **lives in the sea** i.e. is not yet hooked. 91 **clasps** fasten-
ings on the binding (quibble on 'embraces').
  20

Wife. Speak briefly, can you like of Paris' love?

Juliet. I 'll look to like, if looking liking move,   96
But no more deep will I endart mine eye
Than your consent gives strength to make it fly.

Enter Servingman.

Servingman. Madam, the guests are come, supper serv'd up, you call'd, my young lady ask'd for, the Nurse curs'd in the pantry, and everything in extremity. I must hence to wait, I beseech you follow straight.   [*Exit.*]

Wife. We follow thee. Juliet, the County stays.

Nurse. Go girl, seek happy nights to happy days.
                                        Exeunt.

[SCENE 4]

*Enter Romeo, Mercutio, Benvolio, with five or six
other Maskers, Torchbearers.*

Romeo. What! shall this speech be spoke for our
                excuse,
Or shall we on without apology?

Benvolio. The date is out of such prolixity.
We 'll have no Cupid hoodwink'd with a scarf,
Bearing a Tartar's painted bow of lath,   5
Scaring the ladies like a crowkeeper,
⟨Nor no without-book prologue, faintly spoke

95 **like of** be pleased with. 96 **look** be prepared. 98 **it** Q1; Q2 omits. 99 **the guests are come** N. 101 **in extremity** at the breaking point. 103 **straight** immediately. 104 **stays** waits. SD **Mercutio** N. **Torchbearers** N. 1 **this speech** N. 4 **hoodwink'd** blindfolded. 5 **Tartar's painted bow** N. **of lath** i.e. imitation. 6 **crowkeeper** boy archer employed as scarecrow. 7–8 ⟨Nor . . . entrance⟩ N. 7 **without-book** memorized. **prologue** see The Prologue N.

21

After the prompter, for our entrance).
But let them measure us by what they will,
We 'll measure them a measure and be gone.   10
   Romeo. Give me a torch! I am not for this ambling.
Being but heavy, I will bear the light.
   Mercutio. Nay gentle Romeo, we must have you
      dance.
   Romeo. Not I, believe me. You have dancing shoes
With nimble soles, I have a soul of lead   15
So stakes me to the ground I cannot move.
   Mercutio. You are a lover, borrow Cupid's wings
And soar with them above a common bound.
   Romeo. I am too sore enpierced with his shaft
To soar with his light feathers, and so bound   20
I cannot bound a pitch above dull woe.
Under love's heavy burthen do I sink.
   Mercutio. And to sink in it should you burthen
      love—
Too great oppression for a tender thing.
   Romeo. Is love a tender thing? it is too rough,   25
Too rude, too boist'rous, and it pricks like thorn.
   Mercutio. If love be rough with you, be rough with
      love:
Prick love for pricking and you beat love down.
Give me a case to put my visage in.
A visor for a visor! what care I   30
What curious eye doth cote deformities?
Here are the beetle brows shall blush for me.

8 **After** with assistance from. **entrance** here trisyllabic. 9 **measure us** find out about us. 10 **measure them a measure** dance with them a stately dance. 11 **ambling** dancing (compared to a horse's gait). 12–21 **heavy . . . bound** N. 21 **pitch** height reached by a falcon before swooping on its prey. 29 **case** mask. 30 **A . . . visor** a mask for a masklike face. 31 **cote** quote, observe. 32 **shall** that shall.

Benvolio. Come, knock and enter, and no sooner in
But every man betake him to his legs.

Romeo. A torch for me! let wantons light of heart
Tickle the senseless rushes with their heels,   36
For I am proverb'd with a grandsire phrase—
I 'll be a candle-holder and look on.
The game was ne'er so fair, and I am dun.

Mercutio. Tut, dun 's the mouse, the constable's own
      word.   40
If thou are Dun we 'll draw thee from the mire
Of (save your reverence) love, wherein thou stick'st
Up to the ears. Come, we burn daylight, ho!

Romeo. Nay that 's not so.

Mercutio.   I mean, sir, in delay
We waste our lights in vain. Lights, lights by day!
Take our good meaning, for our judgment sits   46
Five times in that ere once in our five wits.

Romeo. And we mean well in going to this mask,
But 'tis no wit to go.

Mercutio.   Why? may one ask.

Romeo. I dreamt a dream tonight.

Mercutio.   And so did I.

Romeo. Well, what was yours?

Mercutio.   That dreamers often lie.   51

35 **wantons** triflers. 36 **rushes** the usual floor-covering before car-
pets. 37 **proverb'd . . . phrase** supplied with an old man's proverb N. 38 **candle-holder** onlooker. 39 **game** quarry (quibble on
'gambling'). **dun** Q2 *dum;* Q1 *done;* dark, ugly (pun on 'done,'
finished) N. 40 **dun's the mouse** keep quiet, lie low (proverbial).
constable's own word i.e. when lying in wait for an arrest. 41
Dun proverbial name for a horse N. 42 **Of** Q1; Q2 *Or.* **save your
reverence** begging your pardon. 43 **burn daylight** waste time.
44 **Nay** Romeo quibbles on 'waste torchlight by day.' **not so**
since it is now after dark. 46 **good** correct. 46–7 **judgment . . .
wits** N. 47 **five wits** Q2 *fine wits.* 48 **mask** masking party. 49 **no
wit** unwise. 50 **tonight** last night.

Romeo. In bed asleep while they do dream things
    true.

Mercutio. O, then I see Queen Mab hath been with
    you.

She is the fairies' midwife, and she comes
In shape no bigger than an agate stone   55
On the forefinger of an alderman,
Drawn with a team of little *atomi*
Over men's noses as they lie asleep;
Her wagon spokes made of long spinners' legs,
The cover of the wings of grasshoppers,   60
Her traces of the smallest spider web,
Her collars of the moonshine's wat'ry beams,
Her whip of cricket's bone, the lash of philome,
Her wagoner a small grey-coated gnat
Not half so big as a round little worm   65
Prick'd from the lazy finger of a maid;
Her chariot is an empty hazel nut,
Made by the joiner squirrel or old grub,
Time out a mind the fairies' coachmakers.
And in this state she gallops night by night   70
Through lovers' brains and then they dream of love,
On courtiers' knees that dream on cursies straight,
O'er lawyers' fingers who straight dream on fees,
O'er ladies' lips who straight on kisses dream,
Which oft the angry Mab with blisters plagues   75
Because their breaths with sweetmeats tainted are.
Sometime she gallops o'er a courtier's nose

53, 54 **Queen Mab, midwife** N. 54–91 **She is . . . bodes** prose
in Q2; verse in Q1. 55 **agate stone** N. 57 **atomi** Q1; Q2 *ottamie*;
atoms, tiny creatures N. 59 **spinners** spiders. 62 **wat'ry** since the
moon was thought to cause dew. 63 **philome** film, gossamer. 65
worm idleness was supposed to breed maggots in the fingers.
66 **maid** Q1; Q2 *man* N. 68 **joiner** cabinetmaker. 69 **a** of. 70 **state**
pomp. 72 **cursies** curtsies. 76 **sweetmeats** kissing-comfits (for
perfuming the breath).

24

And then dreams he of smelling out a suit,
And sometime comes she with a tithe-pig's tail
Tickling a parson's nose as 'a lies asleep—   80
Then he dreams of another benefice.
Sometime she driveth o'er a soldier's neck
And then dreams he of cutting foreign throats,
Of breaches, ambuscadoes, Spanish blades,
Of healths five fadom deep; and then anon   85
Drums in his ear, at which he starts and wakes,
And being thus frighted swears a prayer or two
And sleeps again. This is that very Mab
That plats the manes of horses in the night
And bakes the elflocks in foul sluttish hairs   90
Which once entangled much misfortune bodes.
This is the hag, when maids lie on their backs,
That presses them and learns them first to bear,
Making them women of good carriage.
This is she—
   Romeo.   Peace, peace, Mercutio, peace!   95
Thou talk'st of nothing.
   Mercutio.   True, I talk of dreams,
Which are the children of an idle brain,
Begot of nothing but vain phantasy,
Which is as thin of substance as the air
And more inconstant than the wind, who woos   100
E'en now the frozen bosom of the North,
And being anger'd puffs away from thence,
Turning his face to the dew-dropping South.

78 **suit** N. 79 **tithe-pig** every tenth pig born (due the parson as
church tax). 80 **'a** he. 84 **ambuscadoes** ambushes. 85 **fadom**
fathoms (old plural). **anon** presently. 90 **elflocks** cakes of tangled
hair (supposedly the work of elves). 91 **entangled** Q2 *vntangled*
92 **hag** incubus. 93 **bear** bear children (quibble on 'support a
man'). 94 **carriage** here pronounced 'carri-age' N. 97 **idle** empty
98 **phantasy** imagination. 103 **face** Q1; Q2 *side*.

25

Benvolio. This wind you talk of blows us from our-
    selves.
Supper is done, and we shall come too late.   105
  Romeo. I fear too early, for my mind misgives
Some consequence yet hanging in the stars
Shall bitterly begin his fearful date
With this night's revels, and expire the term
Of a despised life clos'd in my breast   110
By some vile forfeit of untimely death.
But He that hath the stirrage of my course
Direct my sail. On, lusty gentlemen.
  Benvolio. Strike drum.   114

*They march about the stage, and Servingmen
come forth with napkins.*

  1. Servingman. Where 's Potpan that he helps not
to take away? He shift a trencher! he scrape a
trencher!
  2. Servingman. When good manners shall lie all in
one or two men's hands, and they unwash'd too, 'tis
a foul thing.   120
  1. Servingman. Away with the join-stools, remove
the court-cubbert, look to the plate. Good thou, save
me a piece of marchpane, and as thou loves me let
the porter let in Susan Grindstone and Nell. An-
thony and Potpan!   125
  3. Servingman. Ay boy, ready.
  1. Servingman. You are look'd for and call'd for,
ask'd for and sought for in the great chamber.

104 **ourselves** i.e. our present intentions. 107 **consequence** future
event. 108 **his** its. **date** period, duration. 109–11 **expire . . . death**
N. 112 **stirrage** steerage. 113 **sail** Q1; Q2 *sute.* SD **They march
. . . napkins** for staging see N. 115–31 **Where 's Potpan . . .
take all** N. 116 **trencher** wooden platter. 121 **join** fabricated by a
joiner. 122 **court-cubbert** court-cupboard, sideboard. **plate** table-
ware. 123 **marchpane** marzipan (an almond candy). 128 **great
chamber** hall used for social occasions.

4. Servingman. We cannot be here and there too.
Cheerly, boys, be brisk awhile and the longer liver
take all.   *Exeunt [Servingmen].*

*Enter ⟨old Capulet with⟩ all the Guests and
Gentlewomen to the Maskers.*

Capulet. Welcome gentlemen, ladies that have their
    toes
Unplagu'd with corns will walk a bout with you.
Ah my mistresses, which of you all   134
Will now deny to dance? She that makes dainty,
She I 'll swear hath corns. Am I come near ye now?
Welcome gentlemen, I have seen the day
That I have worn a visor and could tell
A whispering tale in a fair lady's ear   139
Such as would please. 'Tis gone, 'tis gone, 'tis gone.
You are welcome, gentlemen. Come musicians, play.
                    Music plays and they dance.
A hall, a hall! give room! And foot it, girls.
More light! you knaves, and turn the tables up,
And quench the fire, the room is grown too hot.
Ah sirrah, this unlook'd-for sport comes well.   145
Nay sit, nay sit, good cousin Capulet,
For you and I are past our dancing days.
How long is 't now since last yourself and I
Were in a mask?
2. Capulet.   Berlady, thirty years.

130 the longer . . . all i.e. let's be cheerfully resigned (proverbial). SD Enter . . . to the Maskers N. 133 walk a bout tread
a measure. a bout Q2 *about*. 135 makes dainty affects fastidious-
ness. 136 Am I . . . now? Have I hit the truth? 142 A hall clear
the floor. 143 knaves fellows. tables hinged leaves on trestles.
145 sirrah here used familiarly. 146 cousin used of any but nearest
relatives. cousin Capulet probably Capulet's uncle (see I.2.70).
149 Were in i.e. wore. Berlady By our Lady (the Virgin Mary).

Capulet. What! man, 'tis not so much, 'tis not so
    much,   150
'Tis since the nuptial of Lucentio
(Come Pentecost as quickly as it will)
Some five and twenty years, and then we mask'd.
  2. Capulet. 'Tis more, 'tis more, his son is elder, sir,
His son is thirty.
  Capulet.   Will you tell me that?   155
His son was but a ward two years ago.
  Romeo. What lady 's that which doth enrich the
    hand
Of yonder knight?
  Servant. I know not, sir.   159
  Romeo. O she doth teach the torches to burn bright.
It seems she hangs upon the cheek of night
As a rich jewel in an Ethiop's ear—
Beauty too rich for use, for earth too dear.
So shows a snowy dove trooping with crows
As yonder lady o'er her fellows shows.   165
The measure done, I 'll watch her place of stand,
And touching hers make blessed my rude hand.
Did my heart love till now? forswear it, Sight!
For I ne'er saw true beauty till this night.   169
  Tybalt. This by his voice should be a Montague.
Fetch me my rapier, boy. What! dares the slave
Come hither cover'd with an antic face
To fleer and scorn at our solemnity?
Now by the stock and honor of my kin,
To strike him dead I hold it not a sin.   175
  Capulet. Why, how now! kinsman, wherefore storm
    you so?

151 **nuptial** wedding. 152 **Pentecost** Whitsunday (seventh Sunday
after Easter). 156 **ward** minor in charge of a guardian. 164 **shows**
appears. 171 **slave** base fellow. 172 **antic face** grotesque mask.
173 **fleer** sneer. **solemnity** festivity.
  28

Tybalt. Uncle, this is a Montague, our foe,
A villain that is hither come in spite
To scorn at our solemnity this night.
  Capulet. Young Romeo is it?   180
  Tybalt. 'Tis he, that villain Romeo.
  Capulet. Content thee, gentle coz, let him alone.
'A bears him like a portly gentleman,
And, to say truth, Verona brags of him
To be a virtuous and well-govern'd youth.   185
I would not for the wealth of all this town
Here in my house do him disparagement.
Therefore be patient, take no note of him.
It is my will, the which if thou respect,
Show a fair presence and put off these frowns,   190
An ill-beseeming semblance for a feast.
  Tybalt. It fits when such a villain is a guest,
I 'll not endure him.
  Capulet.   He shall be endur'd.
What! goodman boy, I say he shall. Go to!
Am I the master here or you? Go to!   195
You 'll not endure him! God shall mend my soul,
You 'll make a mutiny among my guests!
You will set cock-a-hoop! You 'll be the man!
  Tybalt. Why Uncle, 'tis a shame.
  Capulet.   Go to, go to!
You are a saucy boy. [*Aside.*] Is 't so indeed?   200
This trick may chance to scathe you. I know what,
You must contrary me! Marry, 'tis time—

---

182 **Content thee** calm thyself. 183 **portly** of good deportment,
well mannered. 187 **disparagement** indignity. 188 **patient** calm,
forbearing. 190 **presence** demeanor. 194 **goodman boy** a contemp-
tuous phrase N. **Go to** get out. 196 **mend** amend, purge, save.
197 **mutiny** disturbance. 198 **set cock-a-hoop** be utterly reckless
N. 200 SD **Aside** N. 201 **trick** i.e. of brawling. **scathe** harm.
202 **contrary** stressed — ´ —.

Well said, my hearts. You are a princox, go!
Be quiet or— More light, more light! For shame!
I 'll make you quiet— What! cheerly, my hearts. 205
   Tybalt. Patience perforce with willful choler meeting
Makes my flesh tremble in their diff'rent greeting.
I will withdraw, but this intrusion shall,
Now seeming sweet, convert to bitt'rest gall. *Exit.*
   Romeo. If I profane with my unworthiest hand
This holy shrine, the gentle sin is this, 211
My lips, two blushing pilgrims, ready stand
To smooth that rough touch with a tender kiss.
   Juliet. Good pilgrim, you do wrong your hand too
    much,
Which mannerly devotion shows in this, 215
For saints have hands that pilgrims hands do touch,
And palm to palm is holy palmers' kiss.
   Romeo. Have not saints lips and holy palmers too?
   Juliet. Ay pilgrim, lips that they must use in
    prayer.
   Romeo. O then dear saint, let lips do what hands
    do— 220
They pray, grant thou, lest faith turn to despair.
   Juliet. Saints do not move, though grant for pray-
    ers' sake.
   Romeo. Then move not while my prayer's effect I
    take.

203 **princox** coxcomb, conceited youth. 206 **Patience perforce** enforced self-control (proverbial). 207 **diff'rent** hostile. **greeting** encounter. 210–23 **If I profane . . . I take** the lovers' first dialogue forms a sonnet. 211 **shrine** i.e. Juliet's hand. 211–13 **the gentle sin . . . kiss** N. 212–17 **pilgrims . . . palmers** N. 212 **ready** Q1; Q2 *did readie;* for text see V.3.102 N. 215 **mannerly** well mannered, polite. 216 **saints** images of saints. 222 **move . . . sake** initiate action, though they do answer prayers. 223 **effect** fulfillment.

Thus from my lips, by thine, my sin is purg'd.

Juliet. Then have my lips the sin that they have
    took. 225

Romeo. Sin from my lips? O trespass sweetly urg'd!
Give me my sin again.

Juliet.   You kiss by th' book.

Nurse. Madam, your mother craves a word with
    you.

Romeo. What is her mother?

Nurse.   Marry bachelor,
Her mother is the lady of the house, 230
And a good lady, and a wise and virtuous.
I nurs'd her daughter that you talk'd withal.
I tell you, he that can lay hold of her
Shall have the chinks.

Romeo.   Is she a Capulet?
O dear account! my life is my foe's debt. 235

Benvolio. Away, be gone, the sport is at the best.

Romeo. Ay, so I fear, the more is my unrest.

Capulet. Nay gentlemen, prepare not to be gone,
We have a trifling foolish banquet towards.

                   ⟨*They whisper in his ear.*⟩

Is it e'en so? why then I thank you all. 240
I thank you, honest gentlemen. Good night.
More torches here! Come on then, let's to bed.
Ah, sirrah, by my fay, it waxes late,
I'll to my rest.

        ⟨*Exeunt* [*Capulet and most of the others.*]⟩

---

224 Thus . . . purg'd N. 226 urg'd mentioned. 227 by th' book
authoritatively. 229 What who. 232 withal with. 234 the chinks
plenty of coin. 235 dear grievous (quibble on 'costly'). is my
foe's debt is owed to my foe (i.e. is in Juliet's power). 239 foolish
humble. banquet refreshments, supper. towards in preparation.
241 honest honorable 243 fay faith.

Juliet. Come hither, Nurse. What is yond gentle-
man?   245
Nurse. The son and heir of old Tiberio.
Juliet. What 's he that now is going out of door?
Nurse. Marry, that I think be young Petruchio.
Juliet. What 's he that follows here that would not
dance?
Nurse. I know not.   250
Juliet. Go ask his name. If he be married
My grave is like to be my wedding bed.
Nurse. His name is Romeo, and a Montague,
The only son of your great enemy.   254
Juliet. My only love sprung from my only hate!
Too early seen unknown, and known too late!
Prodigious birth of love it is to me
That I must love a loathed enemy.
Nurse. What 's this? what 's this?
Juliet.   A rhyme I learn'd e'en now
Of one I danc'd withal.

One calls within, 'Juliet!'
Nurse.   Anon, anon!   260
Come, let 's away, the strangers all are gone.   *Exeunt.*

[*Enter Chorus.*]

CHORUS. *Now old Desire doth in his deathbed lie,*
And young Affection gapes to be his heir.
That fair for which Love groan'd for and would die,
With tender Juliet match'd, is now not fair.   265
Now Romeo is belov'd and loves again,

---

248 **be** may be (subjunctive). **Petruchio** N. 255 **sprung** descended.
257 **Prodigious** monstrous, ill-omened. 260 **Anon** right away.
262–75 **Now old Desire . . . sweet** N. 262 **old Desire** i.e. for
Rosaline. 263 **gapes** is eager. 264 **Love** i.e. the lover.

Alike bewitched by the charm of looks;
But to his foe suppos'd he must complain,
And she steal love's sweet bait from fearful hooks.
Being held a foe, he may not have access   270
To breathe such vows as lovers use to swear;
And she, as much in love, her means much less
To meet her new beloved anywhere.
But passion lends them pow'r, time means, to meet,
Temp'ring extremities with extreme sweet.   [*Exit.*]

267 **Alike** i.e. both he and she. 275 **extremities** hardships. **extreme** stressed ´ –.

33

[*Act II*

SCENE 1]

Enter Romeo alone.

Romeo. Can I go forward when my heart is here?
Turn back, dull earth, and find thy center out.

[Retires.]

Enter Benvolio with Mercutio.

Benvolio. Romeo, my cousin Romeo! Romeo!
Mercutio. He 's wise and on my life hath stol'n
    him home to bed.
Benvolio. He ran this way and leapt this orchard
    wall.   5
Call, good Mercutio.
Mercutio.   Nay I 'll conjure too.
Romeo! humors! madman! passion! lover!
Appear thou in the likeness of a sigh,
Speak but one rhyme and I am satisfy'd,   9
Cry but 'Ay me!' pronounce but 'love' and 'dove,'
Speak to my goship Venus one fair word,
One nickname for her purblind son and heir,

1 **forward** i.e. away from Juliet. 2 **earth** . . . **center** body . . .
heart N. SD **Retires** i.e. hides behind a pillar or stage property.
4 **He 's** N. 6 **conjure** call up a spirit by incantation. 7 **Romeo** . . .
lover N. **humors** moods, whims. 8 **in** . . . **sigh** in form of mist.
10 **pronounce** Q1; Q2 *prouaunt.* **dove** Q1; Q2 *day.* 11 **goship** gossip,
friend, confidant. 12 **purblind** totally blind. **heir** Q1; Q2 *her.*

34

Young Abram Cupid, he that shot so true
When King Cophetua lov'd the beggar maid.
He heareth not, he stirreth not, he moveth not: 15
The ape is dead and I must conjure him.
I conjure thee by Rosaline's bright eyes,
By her high forehead and her scarlet lip,
By her fine foot, straight leg and quiv'ring thigh,
And the demesnes that there adjacent lie,   20
That in thy likeness thou appear to us.
  Benvolio. And if he hear thee thou wilt anger him.
  Mercutio. This cannot anger him. 'Twould anger
    him
To raise a spirit in his mistress' circle
Of some strange nature, letting it there stand   25
Till she had laid it and conjur'd it down—
That were some spite. My invocation
Is fair and honest, in his mistress' name
I conjure only but to raise up him.
  Benvolio. Come, he hath hid himself among these
    trees   30
To be consorted with the hum'rous night.
Blind is his love and best befits the dark.
  Mercutio. If love be blind love cannot hit the mark.
Now will he sit under a medlar tree
And wish his mistress were that kind of fruit   35
As maids call medlars when they laugh alone.

13 **Abram** beggarly, hypocritical (like an Abraham Man) N. 14
King Cophetua a ballad character N. 16 **dead** playing dead (like
a performing ape). **conjure him** i.e. to raise his ghost. 24 **circle**
magic ring (quibble on 'pudendum'). 25 **strange** belonging to another person. 26 **conjur'd** stressed − ⌣. 27 **spite** injury **invocation**
here five syllables; see I.4.94 N. 31 **consorted** associated. **hum'rous**
moist (quibble on 'moody'). 34 **medlar** a fruit resembling a small
brown apple (symbol of pudendum).

O Romeo, that she were— O that she were
An open-arse or thou a pop'rin pear.
Romeo, good night. I 'll to my truckle-bed,
This field-bed is too cold for me to sleep.   40
Come, shall we go?

 Benvolio.   Go then, for 'tis in vain
To seek him here that means not to be found.

       Exeunt [*Benvolio and Mercutio*].

 Romeo. He jests at scars that never felt a wound.
But soft, what light through yonder window breaks?
It is the East and Juliet is the sun.   45
Arise fair Sun and kill the envious Moon,
Who is already sick and pale with grief
That thou her maid art far more fair than she.
Be not her maid, since she is envious,
Her vestal liv'ry is but sick and green,   50
And none but fools do wear it, cast it off.

[*Enter Juliet at the window.*]

It is my lady! O it is my love!
O that she knew she were!
She speaks yet she says nothing, what of that?
Her eye discourses, I will answer it.   55
I am too bold, 'tis not to me she speaks.
Two of the fairest stars in all the heaven,
Having some business, do entreat her eyes
To twinkle in their spheres till they return.
What if her eyes were there, they in her head?   60

38 **open-arse** Q2 *open;* Q1 *open Et cœtera;* medlar N. **pop'rin pear**
N. 39 **truckle-bed** a low bed trundled by day under a standing
bed. 40 **field-bed** bed on the bare ground. 43 **Romeo** for staging
see N. 44 **soft** hush. 46 **moon** Diana (goddess of chastity).
50 **vestal** virgin. **green** pale, sickly (as from green-sickness;
compare III.5.156). SD **Enter . . . window** N. **window** N. 57
stars planets. 58 **do** Q1; Q2 *to.* 59 **spheres** orbits N.

The brightness of her cheek would shame those stars
As daylight doth a lamp; her eye in heaven
Would through the airy region stream so bright
That birds would sing and think it were not night.
See how she leans her cheek upon her hand!   65
O that I were a glove upon that hand
That I might touch that cheek.

 Juliet.   Ay me!

 Romeo.   She speaks.

O speak again, bright angel, for thou art
As glorious to this night, being o'er my head,
As is a winged messenger of Heaven   70
Unto the white-upturned wond'ring eyes
Of mortals that fall back to gaze on him
When he bestrides the lazy puffing clouds
And sails upon the bosom of the air.   74

 Juliet. O Romeo, Romeo, wherefore art thou Romeo?
Deny thy father and refuse thy name;
Or if thou wilt not, be but sworn my love
And I 'll no longer be a Capulet.

 Romeo. Shall I hear more or shall I speak at this?

 Juliet. 'Tis but thy name that is my enemy,   80
Thou art thyself, though not a Montague.
What 's Montague? it is nor hand nor foot
Nor arm nor face, O be some other name
Belonging to a man.
What 's in a name? that which we call a rose   85
By any other word would smell as sweet.
So Romeo would, were he not Romeo call'd,
Retain that dear perfection which he owes
Without that title. Romeo, doff thy name,

---

63 stream shine. 73 puffing up-swelling, inflating N. 75 wherefore
why. 81 though not even if thou wert not. 82–4 What 's Montague
. . . a man N. 88 owes owns.

37

And for thy name, which is no part of thee,   90
Take all myself.

   Romeo.   I take thee at thy word.
Call me but Love and I 'll be new baptiz'd,
Henceforth I never will be Romeo.

   Juliet. What man art thou that thus bescreen'd in
      night
So stumblest on my counsel?

   Romeo.   By a name   95
I know not how to tell thee who I am.
My name, dear saint, is hateful to myself
Because it is an enemy to thee.
Had I it written, I would tear the word.   99

   Juliet. My ears have yet not drunk a hundred words
Of thy tongue's utt'ring, yet I know the sound.
Art thou not Romeo, and a Montague?

   Romeo. Neither, fair maid, if either thee dislike.

   Juliet. How cam'st thou hither, tell me, and where-
      fore?
The orchard walls are high and hard to climb,   105
And the place death, considering who thou art,
If any of my kinsmen find thee here.

   Romeo. With Love's light wings did I o'erperch
      these walls,
For stony limits cannot hold Love out,   109
And what Love can do, that dares Love attempt.
Therefore thy kinsmen are no stop to me.

   Juliet. If they do see thee they will murther thee.

   Romeo. Alack, there lies more peril in thine eye
Than twenty of their swords, look thou but sweet
And I am proof against their enmity.   115

---

95 **counsel** secret thought. 99 **written** in writing. 103 **dislike** displease. 108 **o'erperch** fly over. 111 **stop** obstacle. 115 **proof** armored.

Juliet. I would not for the world they saw thee here.

Romeo. I have night's cloak to hide me from their eyes,

And but thou love me, let them find me here.

My life were better ended by their hate

Than death prorogued, wanting of thy love.   120

Juliet. By whose direction found'st thou out this place?

Romeo. By Love, that first did prompt me to inquire.

He lent me counsel, and I lent him eyes.

I am no pilot, yet wert thou as far

As that vast shore wash'd with the farthest sea,   125

I should adventure for such marchandise.

Juliet. Thou know'st the mask of night is on my face,

Else would a maiden blush bepaint my cheek

For that which thou hast heard me speak tonight.

Fain would I dwell on form—fain, fain deny   130

What I have spoke. But farewell compliment.

Dost thou love me? I know thou wilt say 'Ay,'

And I will take thy word. Yet if thou swear'st

Thou mayst prove false—at lovers' perjuries

They say Jove laughs. O gentle Romeo,   135

If thou dost love pronounce it faithfully—

Or if thou think'st I am too quickly won,

I 'll frown and be perverse and say thee nay,

So thou wilt woo; but else, not for the world.

In truth, fair Montague, I am too fond,   140

And therefore thou mayst think my havior light,

---

118 **but** unless. 120 **prorogued** postponed. 126 **adventure** take the risk (of searching). 130 **Fain** gladly. 131 **compliment** convention. 139 **So** provided that. 140 **fond** foolishly affectionate. 141 **havior** Q1; Q2 *behavior*. **light** immodest.

But trust me, gentleman, I 'll prove more true
Than those that have more cunning to be strange.
I should have been more strange, I must confess,
But that thou overheard'st, ere I was ware,   145
My true-love passion. Therefore pardon me,
And not impute this yielding to light love,
Which the dark night hath so discovered.

  Romeo. Lady, by yonder blessed moon I vow,
That tips with silver all these fruit-tree tops—   150

  Juliet. O swear not by the moon, th' inconstant
  moon,
That monthly changes in her circl'd orb,
Lest that thy love prove likewise variable.

  Romeo. What shall I swear by?

  Juliet.   Do not swear at all,
Or if thou wilt, swear by thy gracious self,   155
Which is the god of my idolatry,
And I 'll believe thee.

  Romeo.   If my heart's dear love—

  Juliet. Well, do not swear. Although I joy in thee
I have no joy of this contract tonight.
It is too rash, too unadvis'd, too sudden,   160
Too like the lightning, which doth cease to be
Ere one can say 'It lightens.' Sweet, good night.
This bud of love by Summer's rip'ning breath
May prove a beauteous flow'r when next we meet.
Good night, good night! As sweet repose and rest
Come to thy heart as that within my breast.   166

  Romeo. O wilt thou leave me so unsatisfy'd?

143 **more cunning** Q1; Q2 *coying*. **strange** distant, reserved. 148
Which relates to 'yielding.' **discovered** revealed. 152 **circl'd** Q2
circle; Q1 *circled*. **circl'd orb** the sphere of the moon (see II.1.
59 N). 159 **contract** exchange of vows (stressed – ⌣) N. 160
unadvis'd unconsidered.

Juliet. What satisfaction canst thou have tonight?

Romeo. Th' exchange of thy love's faithful vow for
  mine.

Juliet. I gave thee mine before thou didst request it,
And yet I would it were to give again.   171

Romeo. Wouldst thou withdraw it? for what purpose, love?

Juliet. But to be frank and give it thee again.
And yet I wish but for the thing I have,
My bounty is as boundless as the sea,   175
My love as deep—the more I give to thee
The more I have, for both are infinite.
I hear some noise within. Dear love, adieu—
                              [*Nurse calls within.*]
Anon, good Nurse! Sweet Montague, be true.   179
Stay but a little, I will come again.   [*Exit.*]

Romeo. O blessed blessed night! I am afear'd,
Being in night, all this is but a dream
Too flatt'ring sweet to be substantial.

[*Enter Juliet again.*]

Juliet. Three words, dear Romeo, and good night
  indeed.
If that thy bent of love be hon'rable,   185
Thy purpose marriage, send me word tomorrow
By one that I 'll procure to come to thee
Where and what time thou wilt perform the rite,
And all my fortunes at thy foot I 'll lay
And follow thee my lord throughout the world.   190

Nurse. [*Within.*] Madam!

173 **frank** free-handed, generous. **SD within** off stage. 183 **sub-**
stantial real; here pronounced 'substanti-al'; see I.4.94 N. 185
thy bent of love the object of thy love. 187 **procure** arrange.

Juliet. I come, anon. But if thou mean'st not well,
I do beseech thee—
Nurse. [*Within.*] Madam!
Juliet.   By and by I come.
—To cease thy strife and leave me to my grief.
Tomorrow will I send.   195
Romeo. So thrive my soul.
Juliet.   A thousand times good night.
                                                                      [*Exit.*]
Romeo. A thousand times the worse to want thy
        light!
Love goes toward love as schoolboys from their
        books,
But love from love toward school with heavy looks.

Enter Juliet again.

Juliet. Hist Romeo, hist! O for a falkner's voice
To lure this tassel-gentle back again.   201
Bondage is hoarse and may not speak aloud,
Else would I tear the cave where Echo lies
And make her airy tongue more hoarse than mine
With repetition of my Romeo.   205
Romeo. It is my soul that calls upon my name.
How silver-sweet sound lovers' tongues by night,
Like softest music to attending ears.
Juliet. Romeo—
Romeo.   My dear?
Juliet.   What a clock tomorrow
Shall I send to thee?

191, 193 **Nurse** Q2 omits. **By and by** immediately. 194 **strife**
striving (to woo). 196 **So thrive my soul** as I hope to be saved.
200 **falkner** falconer. 201 **tassel-gentle** tercel-gentle (male pere-
grine falcon). 202 **Bondage is hoarse** i.e. being under my parents'
control I must whisper. 204 **mine** Q2 omits. 208 **attending** listen-
ing. 209 **dear** Q2 *Neece* N.

Romeo.   By the hour of nine.   210
Juliet. I will not fail, 'tis twenty year till then.
I have forgot why I did call thee back.
Romeo. Let me stand here till thou remember it.
Juliet. I shall forget, to have thee still stand there,
Rememb'ring how I love thy company.   215
Romeo. And I 'll still stay, to have thee still forget,
Forgetting any other home but this.
Juliet. 'Tis almost morning. I would have thee gone,
And yet no farther than a wanton's bird
That lets it hop a little from his hand,   220
Like a poor pris'ner in his twisted gyves,
And with a silken threed plucks 't back again,
So loving-jealous of his liberty.
Romeo. I would I were thy bird.
Juliet.   Sweet, so would I,
Yet I should kill thee with much cherishing.   225
Good night, good night!
Romeo.   Parting is such sweet sorrow
That I shall say good night till it be morrow.
Juliet. Sleep dwell upon thine eyes, peace in thy
     breast—   228
Would I were sleep and peace, so sweet to rest!
                        [*Exit.*]
Romeo. The grey-ey'd Morn smiles on the frowning
     Night,
Check'ring the eastern clouds with streaks of light,
And fleckled Darkness like a drunkard reels
From forth Day's path and Titan's burning wheels.

219 **wanton** capricious child. 222 **silken threed** silken thread N.
226 **Romeo** Q2 omits. 226–9 **Good night . . . rest** N. 230 **Romeo**
in Q2 before l. 229. 230–3 **The grey-ey'd Morn . . . wheels** N.
231 **Check'ring** Q1; Q2 *Checking* N; variegating. 232 **fleckled**
dappled. 233 **Titan** i.e. the sun, offspring of the Titan Hyperion.
wheels i.e. of the sun's chariot (compare III.2.1–4).

Hence will I to my ghostly Friar's close cell,   234
His help to crave and my dear hap to tell.   *Exit.*

[SCENE 2]

Enter Friar alone with a basket.

Friar. Now ere the sun advance his burning eye
The day to cheer and night's dank dew to dry,
I must upfill this osier cage of ours
With baleful weeds and precious-juiced flowers.
The Earth that 's Nature's mother is her tomb,   5
What is her burying grave, that is her womb,
And from her womb children of divers kind
We sucking on her natural bosom find,
Many for many virtues excellent,
None but for some and yet all different.   10
O mickle is the powerful grace that lies
In plants, herbs, stones and their true qualities,
For nought so vile that on the earth doth live
But to the earth some special good doth give,   14
Nor ought so good but, strain'd from that fair use,
Revolts from true birth, stumbling on abuse.
Virtue itself turns vice being misapplied,
And vice sometime by action dignified.

Enter Romeo.

Within the infant rind of this weak flower
Poison hath residence and med'cine power,   20

234 **Hence** from here. **ghostly** spiritual, holy. **close** narrow. 235
dear hap good fortune. 1 **advance** raise. 3 **osier cage** willow basket.
11 **mickle** great. **grace** divine power. 15 **strain'd** constrained, per-
verted. SD **Enter Romeo** N.

For this, being smelt, with that part cheers each
    part,
Being tasted, stays all senses with the heart.
Two such opposed kings encamp them still
In man as well as herbs, Grace and rude Will,
And where the worser is predominant   25
Full soon the canker Death eats up that plant.
  Romeo. Good morrow, Father.
  Friar.   *Benedicite!*
What early tongue so sweet saluteth me?
Young son, it argues a distemper'd head
So soon to bid good morrow to thy bed.   30
Care keeps his watch in every old man's eye,
And where Care lodges Sleep will never lie.
But where unbruised Youth with unstuff'd brain
Doth couch his limbs, there golden Sleep doth reign.
Therefore thy earliness doth me assure   35
Thou art uprous'd with some distemp'rature.
Or if not so (then here I hit it right)
Our Romeo hath not been in bed tonight.
  Romeo. That last is true, the sweeter rest was mine.
  Friar. God pardon sin! wast thou with Rosaline?
  Romeo. With Rosaline, my ghostly Father? No.   41
I have forgot that name and that name's woe.
  Friar. That 's my good son. But where hast thou
    been then?
  Romeo. I'll tell thee ere thou ask it me again.
I have been feasting with mine enemy,   45
Where on a sudden one hath wounded me
That 's by me wounded. Both our remedies

21 **that part** its odor. **cheers** revives. **each part** of the body. 22
stays suspends. 24 **Grace** virtue. **Will** desire, lust. 26 **canker**
cankerworm. 27 **Benedicite** God bless you (the final *e* rhymes
with *me*). 29, 36 **distemper'd, distemp'rature** N. 33 **unstuff'd**
empty (of care). 41 **ghostly** spiritual.

Within thy help and holy physic lies.
I bear no hatred, blessed man, for lo
My intercession likewise steads my foe. 50
   Friar. Be plain, good son, and homely in thy drift,
Riddling confession finds but riddling shrift.
   Romeo. Then plainly know my heart's dear love is
     set
On the fair daughter of rich Capulet;
As mine on hers, so hers is set on mine; 55
And all combin'd, save what thou must combine
By holy marriage. When and where and how
We met, we woo'd and made exchange of vow
I 'll tell thee as we pass. But this I pray,
That thou consent to marry us today. 60
   Friar. Holy Saint Francis! what a change is here!
Is Rosaline, that thou didst love so dear,
So soon forsaken? Young men's love then lies
Not truly in their hearts but in their eyes.
Jesu Maria! what a deal of brine 65
Hath wash'd thy sallow cheeks for Rosaline,
How much salt water thrown away in waste
To season love, that of it doth not taste.
The sun not yet thy sighs from heaven clears,
Thy old groans yet ring in mine ancient ears. 70
Lo! here upon thy cheek the stain doth sit
Of an old tear that is not wash'd off yet.
If e'er thou wast thyself and these woes thine,
Thou and these woes were all for Rosaline. 74
And art thou chang'd? Pronounce this sentence then:

48 **physic** healing power (through the sacrament of marriage).
50 **intercession** petition. **steads** benefits. 51 **homely** simple. **drift**
narrative. 52 **shrift** absolution. 56 **combin'd** united. 68 **season**
preserve as by salting (quibble on 'flavor'). 70 **ring** Q2 *ringing*.
72 **yet** the rhyme indicates the common Elizabethan pronunciation 'yit.' 75 **sentence** proverb.

Women may fall when there 's no strength in men.
Romeo. Thou chid'st me oft for loving Rosaline—
Friar. For doting, not for loving, pupil mine.
Romeo. And bad'st me bury love—
Friar.   Not in a grave,
To lay one in another out to have.   80
Romeo. I pray thee chide me not. Her I love now
Doth grace for grace and love for love allow.
The other did not so.
Friar.   O she knew well
Thy love did read by rote that could not spell.
But come, young waverer, come go with me,   85
In one respect I 'll thy assistant be,
For this alliance may so happy prove
To turn your households' rancor to pure love.
Romeo. O let us hence! I stand on sudden haste.
Friar. Wisely and slow, they stumble that run fast.
                                                     Exeunt.

[SCENE 3]

Enter Benvolio and Mercutio.

Mercutio. Where the devil should this Romeo be?
came he not home tonight?
Benvolio. Not to his father's, I spoke with his man.
Mercutio. Why that same pale hard-hearted wench,
that Rosaline, torments him so that he will sure run
mad.   6
Benvolio. Tybalt, the kinsman to old Capulet, hath
sent a letter to his father's house.

---

81 **Her** she whom. 82 **grace** favor. 84 **read** recite. 86 **In one respect**
for one reason. 89 **stand on** insist upon. 1 **should** might. 2 **tonight**
last night. 4–6 **Why . . . run mad** N.

Mercutio. A challenge, on my life.

Benvolio. Romeo will answer it.   10

Mercutio. Any man that can write may answer a letter.

Benvolio. Nay, he will answer the letter's master how he dares, being dared.   14

Mercutio. Alas poor Romeo, he is already dead—stabb'd with a white wench's black eye, run through the ear with a love song, the very pin of his heart cleft with the blind bow-boy's butt-shaft. And is he a man to encounter Tybalt?

Benvolio. Why what is Tybalt?   20

Mercutio. More than Prince of Cats. O he 's the courageous Captain of Compliments. He fights as you sing prick-song—keeps time, distance and proportion. He rests his minim rests—one, two and the third in your bosom. The very butcher of a silk button, a duelist, a duelist! a gentleman of the very first house, of the first and second cause. Ah the immortal *passado!* the *punto reverso!* the *hai!*

Benvolio. The what?   29

Mercutio. The pox of such antic, lisping, affecting fantasticoes. These new tuners of accent! 'By Jesu, a very good blade! a very tall man! a very good

10 **answer** accept. 14 **dared** challenged. 17 **pin** peg holding the mark in the target's center. 18 **bow-boy** Cupid. **butt-shaft** unbarbed arrow for practice at the butts. 21 **Prince of Cats** N. 22 **Compliments** polite formalities. **as you sing prick-song** i.e. precisely (as from written music). 23 **distance** interval. **proportion** rhythm. 24 **minim rests** short pauses (a minim being the shortest note). 25 **butcher . . . button** N. 27 **house** school of fencing. **first and second cause** N. 28 **passado . . . hai** fencing terms N. 30 **antic** absurd. 31 **fantasticoes** Q1; Q2 *phantacies.* **accent** language. 32 **tall** brave.

48

whore!' Why, is not this a lamentable thing, grandsire, that we should be thus afflicted with these
strange flies, these fashion-mongers, these pardon-
me's, who stand so much on the new form that they
cannot sit at ease on the old bench? O their bones,
their bones!   38

Enter Romeo.

Benvolio. Here comes Romeo, here comes Romeo.

Mercutio. Without his roe, like a dried herring. O
flesh, flesh, how art thou fishified! Now is he for
the numbers that Petrarch flowed in. Laura to his
lady was a kitchen wench (marry, she had a better
love to berhyme her!), Dido a dowdy, Cleopatra a
gypsy, Helen and Hero hildings and harlots, Thisbe
a grey eye or so but not to the purpose. Signior
Romeo, *bon jour.* There 's a French salutation to
your French slop. You gave us the counterfeit fairly
last night.   49

Romeo. Good morrow to you both. What counterfeit did I give you?

Mercutio. The slip, sir, the slip, can you not conceive?

Romeo. Pardon, good Mercutio, my business was
great, and in such a case as mine a man may strain
courtesy.   56

33 **grandsire** old man (who would disapprove of affectation).
35 **flies** parasites. **pardon** Q1; Q2 *pardons.* 36 **form** fashion
(quibble on 'bench'). 37 **bones** N. 40 **roe** spawn (quibble on
'sperm'). **like a dried herring** i.e. good-for-nothing. 42 **Laura**
Petrarch's beloved, to whom he addressed his sonnets. 44 **dowdy**
slut. 45 **gypsy** Egyptian (thus of dark complexion). **hildings** good-
for-nothings, baggages. 48 **slop** baggy breeches. 52 **slip** slang for
counterfeit coin. **conceive** understand. 55 **case** quibble on
'pudendum.'

Mercutio. That 's as much as to say, such a case as yours constrains a man to bow in the hams.

Romeo. Meaning, to cursy?

Mercutio. Thou hast most kindly hit it. 60

Romeo. A most courteous exposition.

Mercutio. Nay I am the very pink of courtesy.

Romeo. Pink for flower?

Mercutio. Right.

Romeo. Why then is my pump well flower'd. 65

Mercutio. Sure wit! Follow me this jest now till thou hast worn out thy pump, that when the single sole of it is worn the jest may remain after the wearing solely singular.

Romeo. O single-sol'd jest, solely singular for the singleness! 71

Mercutio. Come between us, good Benvolio, my wits faint.

Romeo. Swits and spurs! swits and spurs! or I 'll cry a match. 75

Mercutio. Nay, if our wits run the wild goose chase, I am done. For thou hast more of the wild goose in one of thy wits than (I am sure) I have in my whole five. Was I with you there for the goose?

Romeo. Thou wast never with me for anything when thou wast not there for the goose. 81

Mercutio. I will bite thee by the ear for that jest.

Romeo. Nay good goose, bite not.

59 **cursy** curtsy. 60 **kindly** naturally, aptly. 65 **flower'd** pinked, perforated (pun on 'floored'). 69 **solely singular** all alone. 70 **single-sol'd** thin, contemptible (quibble on 'souled'). **solely singular** only unique. 71 **singleness** feebleness. 73 **faint** Q2 *faints;* Q1 *faile.* 74 **Swits** switch. **Swits and spurs** i.e. urge your horse faster. 75 **cry a match** claim to have won the contest. 76 **wild goose chase** N. 79 **with you** even with you. 81 **goose** quibble on 'prostitute.' 82 **bite . . . ear** as a sign of affection.

Mercutio. Thy wit is a very bitter sweeting, it is a most sharp sauce.   85

Romeo. And is it not, then, well serv'd in to a sweet goose?

Mercutio. O here 's a wit of cheveril, that stretches from an inch narrow to an ell broad.   89

Romeo. I stretch it out for that word 'broad,' which added to the goose proves thee far and wide a broad goose.   92

Mercutio. Why, is not this better now than groaning for love? Now art thou sociable, now art thou Romeo, now art thou what thou art by Art as well as by Nature, for this driveling love is like a great natural that runs lolling up and down to hide his bauble in a hole.

Benvolio. Stop there, stop there!   99

Mercutio. Thou desirest me to stop in my tale against the hair.

Benvolio. Thou wouldst else have made thy tale large.   103

Mercutio. O thou art deceived! I would have made it short, for I was come to the whole depth of my tale and meant indeed to occupy the argument no longer.   107

Enter Nurse and her Man.

84 **sweeting** sweet-flavored apple. 86 **well serv'd in** sour sauce with sweet meat being proverbial. 88 **cheveril** an elastic leather made from kidskin. 89 **ell** 45 inches. 91 **broad** obvious. 95 **Art** acquired polish. 96 **Nature** inborn ability. 97 **natural** born fool, idiot. 98 **bauble** a court fool's baton or scepter (quibble on 'phallus'). 100 **tale** pun on 'tail.' 101 **against the hair** against the grain (quibble on 'pubic hair'). 103 **large** indecent. 105 **whole** pun on 'hole.' 106 **occupy** quibble on 'copulate' N. SD Enter . . . Man N.

Romeo. Here's goodly gear—a sail, a sail!

Mercutio. Two, two—a shirt and a smock.

Nurse. Peter!   110

Peter. Anon.

Nurse. My fan, Peter.

Mercutio. Good Peter, to hide her face, for her fan's the fairer face.

Nurse. God ye good morrow, gentlemen.   115

Mercutio. God ye good den, fair gentlewoman.

Nurse. Is it good den?

Mercutio. 'Tis no less, I tell ye, for the bawdy hand of the dial is now upon the prick of noon.

Nurse. Out upon you! what a man are you?   120

Romeo. One, gentlewoman, that God hath made, himself to mar.

Nurse. By my troth, it is well said, 'For himself to mar,' quoth 'a? Gentlemen, can any of you tell me where I may find the young Romeo?   125

Romeo. I can tell you, but young Romeo will be older when you have found him than he was when you sought him. I am the youngest of that name, for fault of a worse.

Nurse. You say well.   130

Mercutio. Yea, is the worst well? Very well took, i' faith, wisely, wisely.

Nurse. If you be he, sir, I desire some confidence with you.

108 **goodly gear** i.e. matter for jest (the Nurse). 109 **shirt** i.e. a man. **smock** chemise (i.e. a woman). 110 **Peter** the Nurse's servant. 112 **fan** N. 116 **God ye good den** God give ye good e'en. 119 **prick** point (quibble on 'phallus'). 120 **Out upon you** an expression of indignation. 121 **made** created (quibble on 'caused'; play on 'make' and 'mar'; see I.2.13 N). 123 **By my troth** upon my word. 129 **fault** default, lack. 133 **confidence** malapropism for 'conference.'

Benvolio. She will endite him to some supper!   135
Mercutio. A bawd, a bawd, a bawd! So ho!
Romeo. What hast thou found?
Mercutio. No hare, sir, unless a hare, sir, in a lenten pie, that is something stale and hoar ere it be spent.
⟨*He walks by them and sings.*⟩

> An old hare hoar, and an old hare hoar, is very
>   good meat in Lent,   140
> But a hare that is hoar is too much for a score
>   when it hoars ere it be spent.

Romeo, will you come to your father's? We 'll to dinner thither.
Romeo. I will follow you.   144
Mercutio. Farewell, ancient lady. Farewell, lady.
'Lady, lady—'

           Exeunt ⟨*Benvolio* [*and*] *Mercutio*⟩.
Nurse. I pray you, sir, what saucy merchant was this that was so full of his ropery?
Romeo. A gentleman, Nurse, that loves to hear himself talk, and will speak more in a minute than he will stand to in a month.   151
Nurse. And 'a speak anything against me, I 'll take him down, and 'a were lustier than he is, and twenty such Jacks. And if I cannot I 'll find those that shall. Scurvy knave! I am none of his flirt-jills, I am none of his skains-mates.   ⟨*She turns to Peter her Man.*⟩

---

135 **endite** intentional malapropism for 'invite.' 136 **bawd** go-between. **So ho** the hunter's cry on rousing a hare. 138 **lenten** i.e. without meat. 139 **stale** quibble on 'prostitute.' **hoar** mouldy (pun on 'whore'). **spent** consumed. 146 **'Lady, lady'** from the ballad of 'Chaste Susanna' N. 147 **merchant** chap, fellow. 148 **ropery** rascally talk (worthy of the hangman's rope). 151 **stand to** live up to. 154 **Jacks** knaves. 155 **flirt-jills** flirty wenches. 156 **skains-mates** 'knives'-mates, cut-throats.

And thou must stand by too, and suffer every knave
to use me at his pleasure!   158

Peter. I saw no man use you at his pleasure. If I
had, my weapon should quickly have been out. I warrant you, I dare draw as soon as another man—if I
see occasion in a good quarrel and the law on my
side.   163

Nurse. Now afore God, I am so vex'd that every
part about me quivers. Scurvy knave! Pray you sir,
a word. And as I told you, my young lady bid me
inquire you out. What she bid me say, I will keep to
myself—but first let me tell ye, if ye should lead her
in a fool's paradise (as they say) it were a very
gross kind of behavior (as they say), for the gentlewoman is young, and therefore if you should deal
double with her, truly it were an ill thing to be offer'd
to any gentlewoman and very weak dealing.

Romeo. Nurse, commend me to thy lady and mis-
tress. I protest unto thee—   175

Nurse. Good heart! and i' faith, I will tell her as
much. Lord, Lord, she will be a joyful woman.

Romeo. What wilt thou tell her, Nurse? Thou dost
not mark me.   179

Nurse. I will tell her, sir, that you do protest,
which as I take it is a gentleman-like offer.

Romeo. Bid her devise some means to come to shrift
        this afternoon,
And there she shall at Friar Lawrence' cell
Be shriv'd and marry'd. Here is for thy pains.

Nurse. No truly, sir, not a penny.   185

Romeo. Go to! I say you shall.

Nurse. This afternoon, sir? Well, she shall be there.

172 **double** deceitfully. 173 **weak** contemptible. 174 **commend me**
convey my respects. 175 **protest** declare. 179 **mark** heed. 182 **Bid**
. . . **afternoon** N. 184 **shriv'd** absolved.

Romeo. And stay good Nurse, behind the abbey wall
Within this hour my man shall be with thee
And bring thee cords made like a tackled stair,   190
Which to the high topgallant of my joy
Must be my convoy in the secret night.
Farewell, be trusty and I 'll quit thy pains.
Farewell, commend me to thy mistress.   194

Nurse. Now God in Heaven bless thee! Hark you,
sir.

Romeo. What say'st thou, my dear Nurse?

Nurse. Is your man secret? did you ne'er hear say,
'Two may keep counsel, putting one away'?   199

Romeo. I warrant thee, my man 's as true as steel.

Nurse. Well sir, my mistress is the sweetest lady.
Lord, Lord! when 'twas a little prating thing—O,
there is a nobleman in town, one Paris, that would
fain lay knife aboard, but she, good soul, had as
lieve see a toad, a very toad, as see him. I anger her
sometimes and tell her that Paris is the properer
man, but I 'll warrant you, when I say so she looks
as pale as any clout in the versal world. Doth not
rosemary and Romeo begin both with a letter?   209

Romeo. Ay Nurse, what of that? Both with an *R*.

Nurse. Ah, mocker, that's the dog-name. *R* is for
the— No, I know it begins with some other letter—
and she hath the prettiest sententious of it, of you

190 **tackled stair** rope ladder. 191 **topgallant** the uppermost of
three sections of a mast. 192 **convoy** conveyance. 193 **quit** requite.
194 **mistress** here trisyllabic. 198 **secret** trustworthy. 200 I Q2
omits. 204 **fain** gladly. **lay knife aboard** i.e. as in boarding a vessel.
205 **lieve** lief, gladly. 206 **properer** handsomer. 208 **clout** piece of
cloth. **versal** universal. 209 **rosemary** see IV.4.107 N. **a letter**
the same letter. 211 **dog-name** because the *R* sound suggests a
dog's growling. 213 **sententious** malapropism for 'sentences'
(sayings).

and rosemary, that it would do you good to hear it.
 Romeo. Commend me to thy lady.   ⟨*Exit.*⟩
 Nurse. Ay, a thousand times. Peter!   216
 Peter. Anon.
 Nurse. Before and apace.   *Exeunt.*

[SCENE 4]

Enter Juliet.

 Juliet. The clock struck nine when I did send the
  Nurse,
In half an hour she promis'd to return.
Perchance she cannot meet him—that 's not so.
O she is lame! Love's heralds should be thoughts,
Which ten times faster glides than the sun's beams
Driving back shadows over low'ring hills.   6
Therefore do nimble-pinion'd doves draw Love,
And therefore hath the wind-swift Cupid wings.
Now is the sun upon the highmost hill
Of this day's journey, and from nine till twelve 10
Is three long hours, yet she is not come.
Had she affections and warm youthful blood
She 'ld be as swift in motion as a ball:
My words would bandy her to my sweet love,
And his to me—but old folks, many feign as they
  were dead: 15
Unwieldy, slow, heavy and pale as lead.

Enter Nurse [and Peter].

O God, she comes! O honey Nurse, what news?

218 **apace** quickly. 7 **nimble-pinion'd** swift-winged. **Love** Venus.
12 **affections** natural emotions. 14 **bandy** bat, toss. 15 **And his**
. . . **dead** this line is apparently a fourteener; see II.3.182 N.
  56

Hast thou met with him? Send thy man away.

Nurse. Peter, stay at the gate.   [*Exit Peter.*]

Juliet. Now good sweet Nurse—O Lord, why look'st
    thou sad?   20

Though news be sad, yet tell them merrily;

If good, thou sham'st the music of sweet news

By playing it to me with so sour a face.

Nurse. I am aweary, give me leave awhile.

Fie, how my bones ache! what a jaunce have I!   25

Juliet. I would thou hadst my bones and I thy news.

Nay come, I pray thee, speak! Good, good Nurse,
    speak!

Nurse. Jesu, what haste! can you not stay awhile?

Do you not see that I am out of breath?

Juliet. How art thou out of breath when thou hast
    breath   30

To say to me that thou art out of breath?

Th' excuse that thou dost make in this delay

Is longer than the tale thou dost excuse.

Is thy news good or bad? Answer to that.

Say either, and I 'll stay the circumstance.   35

Let me be satisfy'd, is 't good or bad?

Nurse. Well, you have made a simple choice, you
know not how to choose a man. Romeo? No, not he.
Though his face be better than any man's, yet his leg
excels all men's—and for a hand and a foot and a
body, though they be not to be talk'd on, yet they
are past compare. He is not the flower of courtesy,
but I 'll warrant him as gentle as a lamb. Go thy
ways, wench, serve God. What! have you din'd at
home?   45

Juliet. No, no. But all this did I know before.

24 **leave** permission (to rest). 25 **jaunce** jaunt N. 35 **circumstance**
details. 37 **simple** foolish.

What says he of our marriage, what of that?

Nurse. Lord, how my head aches! what a head
    have I!

It beats as it would fall in twenty pieces.

My back a t'other side—ah, my back, my back! 50

Beshrew your heart for sending me about

To catch my death with jaunging up and down.

Juliet. I' faith, I 'm sorry that thou art not well.

Sweet, sweet, sweet Nurse, tell me, what says my
    love? 54

Nurse. Your love says like an honest gentleman,

And a courteous, and a kind, and a handsome,

And I warrant a virtuous—Where is your mother?

Juliet. Where is my mother? why, she is within.

Where should she be? How oddly thou repliest:

'Your love says like an honest gentleman, 60

"Where is your mother?"'

Nurse.   O God's Lady dear!

Are you so hot? Marry come up, I trow.

Is this the poultice for my aching bones?

Henceforward do your messages yourself. 64

Juliet. Here 's such a coil! Come, what says Romeo?

Nurse. Have you got leave to go to shrift today?

Juliet. I have.

Nurse. Then hie you hence to Friar Lawrence' cell,

There stays a husband to make you a wife.

Now comes the wanton blood up in your cheeks, 70

They 'll be in scarlet straight at any news.

Hie you to church. I must another way,

To fetch a ladder by the which your love

Must climb a bird's nest soon when it is dark.

50 a on 51 **Beshrew** confound. 55 **honest** honorable. 61 **God's
Lady dear** the Virgin Mary. 62 **Marry come up** an expression of
angry impatience. 65 **coil** fuss. 68 **hie** hasten. 70 **wanton** uncon-
trolled. 71 **straight** immediately. 74 **soon** at once.

I am the drudge and toil in your delight,   75
But you shall bear the burthen soon at night.
Go, I'll to dinner. Hie you to the cell.
    Juliet. Hie to high fortune! Honest Nurse, farewell.
                                                    Exeunt.

[SCENE 5]

Enter Friar and Romeo.

    Friar. So smile the Heav'ns upon this holy act
That after-hours with sorrow chide us not!
    Romeo. Amen, amen. But come what sorrow can,
It cannot countervail th' exchange of joy
That one short minute gives me in her sight.   5
Do thou but close our hands with holy words,
Then love-devouring Death do what he dare—
It is enough I may but call her mine.
    Friar. These violent delights have violent ends,
And in their triumph die like fire and powder,   10
Which as they kiss consume. The sweetest honey
Is loathsome in his own deliciousness
And in the taste confounds the appetite.
Therefore love moderately, long love doth so,
Too swift arrives as tardy as too slow.   15

Enter Juliet ⟨somewhat fast and embraceth Romeo⟩.

Here comes the lady. O, so light a foot
Will ne'er wear out the everlasting flint.
A lover may bestride the gossamers
That idles in the wanton summer air,

76 **soon at night** this very night. 3 **what** whatever. 4 **countervail**
counterbalance. 13 **confounds** destroys. 18 **gossamers** spiders'
threads floating on the wind. 19 **wanton** sportive.

And yet not fall, so light is Vanity.   20
   Juliet. Good even to my ghostly confessor.
   Friar. Romeo shall thank thee, daughter, for us
     both.
   Juliet. As much to him, else is his thanks too much.
   Romeo. Ah Juliet, if the measure of thy joy
Be heap'd like mine, and that thy skill be more   25
To blazon it, then sweeten with thy breath
This neighbor air and let rich music's tongue
Unfold th' imagin'd happiness that both
Receive in either by this dear encounter.   29
   Juliet. Conceit, more rich in matter than in words,
Brags of his substance, not of ornament.
They are but beggars that can count their worth,
But my true love is grown to such excess
I cannot sum up sum of half my wealth.
   Friar. Come, come with me, and we will make short
     work,   35
For by your leaves you shall not stay alone
Till Holy Church incorporate two in one.   ⟨*Exeunt.*⟩

20 **Vanity** earthly joy. 21 **confessor** stressed ⌣ – ⌣. 23 **As much**
the same (i.e. 'Good even'). 24 **measure** measuring pot or basket. 25 **that** if. 26 **blazon** describe (as a coat of arms in heraldic
terms). 27 **music's** Q2 *musicke*. 30 **Conceit** understanding. 34 **sum
up sum** add up the total. 37 **Holy Church** see II.1.159 N.

[*Act III*

SCENE 1]

Enter Mercutio, Benvolio and Men.

Benvolio. I pray thee good Mercutio, let 's retire.
The day is hot, the Capels are abroad, and if we
meet we shall not scape a brawl, for now these hot
days is the mad blood stirring.   4

Mercutio. Thou art like one of these fellows that,
when he enters the confines of a tavern, claps me his
sword upon the table and says, 'God send me no
need of thee'—and by the operation of the second
cup draws him on the drawer, when indeed there is
no need.   10

Benvolio. Am I like such a fellow?

Mercutio. Come, come, thou art as hot a Jack in
thy mood as any in Italy, and as soon moved to be
moody and as soon moody to be moved.

Benvolio. And what to?   15

Mercutio. Nay, and there were two such we should
have none shortly, for one would kill the other.
Thou?—why thou wilt quarrel with a man that hath

SD **Men** servants. 1–2 **I pray . . . abroad** for text see II.3.4–6
N. 2 **Capels** stressed $\stackrel{\prime}{-}$ − (see V.1.18). **are** Q1; Q2 omits. 6 **me**
ethical dative. 8 **by . . . cup** when he feels the effect of his
second drink. 9 **draws him** draws his sword. **drawer** tapster,
waiter. 12 **Jack** fellow. 13 **mood** temper. **moved . . . moody** inclined to be angry. 14 **moody . . . moved** angry at being pro-
voked. 16 **and** if.

61

a hair more or a hair less in his beard than thou hast. Thou wilt quarrel with a man for cracking nuts, having no other reason but because thou hast hazel eyes. What eye but such an eye would spy out such a quarrel? Thy head is as full of quarrels as an egg is full of meat, and yet thy head hath been beaten as addle as an egg for quarreling. Thou hast quarrel'd with a man for coughing in the street, because he hath waken'd thy dog that hath lain asleep in the sun. Didst thou not fall out with a tailor for wearing his new doublet before Easter? with another for tying his new shoes with old riband? And yet thou wilt tutor me from quarreling! 31

Benvolio. And I were so apt to quarrel as thou art, any man should buy the fee-simple of my life for an hour and a quarter.

Mercutio. The fee-simple? O simple! 35

Enter Tybalt, Petruchio and others.

Benvolio. By my head, here comes the Capulets.

Mercutio. By my heel, I care not.

Tybalt. Follow me close, for I will speak to them. Gentlemen, good den, a word with one of you. 39

Mercutio. And but one word with one of us? Couple it with something. Make it a word and a blow.

Tybalt. You shall find me apt enough to that, sir, and you will give me occasion.

Mercutio. Could you not take some occasion without giving? 45

21 **reason** pun on 'raisin.' 25 **addle** muddled, confused (quibble on 'rotten'). 29 **doublet** jacket. 30 **riband** ribbon. 33 **fee-simple** possession in perpetuity of land or real property. **for . . . quarter** i.e. for very little. SD **Petruchio** one of Capulet's guests (see I.4.248). 37 **heel** pun on 'heal' (health, salvation).

Tybalt. Mercutio, thou consort'st with Romeo.

Mercutio. Consort? What! dost thou make us minstrels? And thou make minstrels of us, look to hear
nothing but discords. Here 's my fiddlestick, here 's
that shall make you dance. Zounds, consort!   50

Benvolio. We talk here in the public haunt of men.
Either withdraw unto some private place
Or reason coldly of your grievances
Or else depart. Here all eyes gaze on us.

Mercutio. Men's eyes were made to look, and let
them gaze,   55
I will not budge for no man's pleasure, I.

Enter Romeo.

Tybalt. Well, peace be with you, sir, here comes my
man.

Mercutio. But I 'll be hang'd sir, if he wear your
livery.
Marry, go before to field, he 'll be your follower,
Your worship in that sense may call him 'man.'   60

Tybalt. Romeo, the love I bear thee can afford
No better term than this, thou art a villain.

Romeo. Tybalt, the reason that I have to love thee
Doth much excuse the appertaining rage
To such a greeting. Villain am I none,   65
Therefore farewell, I see thou know'st me not.

Tybalt. Boy, this shall not excuse the injuries

46 **consort'st** dost associate (Mercutio quibbles on 'play music
together'). 47 **Consort** company of musicians. 49 **fiddlestick** i.e.
his sword. 50 **Zounds** by God's (i.e. Christ's) wounds. 53 **coldly**
coolly, dispassionately. 58 **livery** Mercutio quibbles on *man* in the
sense of 'servant.' 59 **field** i.e. for dueling. **follower** quibble on
'servant.' 62 **villain** base person. 64 **appertaining . . . To** appropriate . . . to. **rage** i.e. my lack of rage. 67 **Boy** see I.4.194 N.

That thou hast done me, therefore turn and draw.

   Romeo. I do protest I never injur'd thee,
But love thee better than thou canst devise   70
Till thou shalt know the reason of my love.
And so, good Capulet (which name I tender
As dearly as mine own) be satisfy'd.

   Mercutio. O calm, dishon'rable, vile submission!
Alla stoccatho carries it away!   75
Tybalt, you ratcatcher, will you walk?

   Tybalt. What wouldst thou have with me?

   Mercutio. Good King of Cats, nothing but one of
your nine lives, that I mean to make bold withal and
(as you shall use me hereafter) dry-beat the rest of
the eight. Will you pluck your sword out of his
pilcher by the ears? Make haste, lest mine be about
your ears ere it be out.

   Tybalt. I am for you.

   Romeo. Gentle Mercutio, put thy rapier up.   85

   Mercutio. Come sir, your *passado!*   *[They fight.]*

   Romeo. Draw, Benvolio, beat down their weapons.
Gentlemen, for shame forbear this outrage.
Tybalt, Mercutio! the Prince expressly hath
Forbid this bandying in Verona streets.   90
Hold, Tybalt! Good Mercutio!

   ⟨*Tybalt under Romeo's arm thrusts Mercutio in,
and flies.*⟩

   Mercutio. I am hurt.

70 devise imagine. 72 **tender** cherish. 75 **Alla stoccatho** Q2
Alla stucatho N. **carries it away** wins the day. 76, 78 **ratcatcher,
King of Cats** see II.3.21 N. 80 **dry-beat** thrash (without drawing
blood). 82 **pilcher** scabbard (metaphor from 'pilch,' a leather
garment). **ears** i.e. hilt. 86 **passado** see II.3.28 N. 90 **bandying**
exchanging blows, brawling. SD ⟨**Tybalt . . . flies**⟩ Q2 *Away
Tybalt.* **thrusts . . . in** stabs.

A plague a both houses, I am sped.
Is he gone and hath nothing?

Benvolio. What! art thou hurt? 95

Mercutio. Ay, ay, a scratch, a scratch, marry, 'tis
enough.
Where is my page? Go villain, fetch a surgeon.

[Exit Page.]

Romeo. Courage man, the hurt cannot be much. 98

Mercutio. No, 'tis not so deep as a well nor so wide
as a church door, but 'tis enough, 'twill serve—ask
for me tomorrow and you shall find me a grave man.
I am peppered, I warrant, for this world. A plague a
both your houses! Zounds! A dog, a rat, a mouse, a
cat, to scratch a man to death! A braggart, a rogue,
a villain that fights by the book of arithmetic! Why
the devil came you between us? I was hurt under
your arm. 107

Romeo. I thought all for the best.

Mercutio. Help me into some house, Benvolio,
Or I shall faint. A plague a both your houses. 110
They have made worms' meat of me.
I have it, and soundly too. Your houses!

Exeunt [Mercutio and Benvolio].

Romeo. This gentleman, the Prince's near ally,
My very friend, hath got this mortal hurt
In my behalf, my reputation stain'd 115
With Tybalt's slander—Tybalt, that an hour
Hath been my cousin. O sweet Juliet,
Thy beauty hath made me effeminate,
And in my temper soften'd valor's steel. 119

93 **sped** dispatched. 102 **peppered** i.e. finished. 105 **book of arithmetic** rules of fencing theory. 113 **ally** kinsman. 114 **very** true.
119 **temper** state of mind (quibble on 'temper' of steel). **soften'd**
rather than hardened (in the tempering process).

Enter Benvolio.

Benvolio. O Romeo, Romeo, brave Mercutio 's dead.
That gallant spirit hath aspir'd the clouds,
Which too untimely here did scorn the earth.

 Romeo. This day's black fate on moe days doth
  depend,
This but begins the woe others must end.

⟨*Enter Tybalt.*⟩

 Benvolio. Here comes the furious Tybalt back
  again.   125

 Romeo. He gay in triumph, and Mercutio slain!
Away to Heav'n, respective lenity,
And fire-ey'd Fury be my conduct now!
Now Tybalt, take the 'villain' back again
That late thou gav'st me, for Mercutio's soul 130
Is but a little way above our heads,
Staying for thine to keep him company.
Either thou or I or both must go with him.

 Tybalt. Thou wretched boy that didst consort him
  here
Shalt with him hence.

 Romeo.   This shall determine that. 135
        They fight. Tybalt falls.

 Benvolio. Romeo, away, be gone!
The Citizens are up and Tybalt slain.
Stand not amaz'd, the Prince will doom thee death

---

120 **brave** noble, excellent. 121 **aspir'd** mounted to. 123 **moe** more
(in number). **depend** impend, hang over. 126 **He gay** Q2 *He gan;*
Q1 *A liue* N. 127 **respective** considerate (of Tybalt's blood-tie
with Juliet). 128 **ey'd** Q1; Q2 *end.* **conduct** conductor, guide. 135
This i.e. his sword. 137 **up** up in arms. 138 **amaz'd** confounded.
doom condemn to.

If thou art taken. Hence, be gone, away! 139
  Romeo. O I am Fortune's fool!
  Benvolio.   Why dost thou stay?
                                 Exit Romeo.

Enter Citizens.

  Citizens. Which way ran he that kill'd Mercutio?
Tybalt, that murtherer, which way ran he?
  Benvolio. There lies that Tybalt.
  Citizen.   Up sir, go with me.
I charge thee in the Prince's name obey. 144

Enter Prince, old Montague, Capulet, their Wives and all.

  Prince. Where are the vile beginners of this fray?
  Benvolio. O noble Prince, I can discover all
Th' unlucky manage of this fatal brawl.
There lies the man, slain by young Romeo,
That slew thy kinsman, brave Mercutio.
  Capulet's Wife. Tybalt, my cousin! O my brother's
    child! 150
O Prince! O husband! O the blood is spill'd
Of my dear kinsman! Prince, as thou art true,
For blood of ours shed blood of Montague.
O cousin, cousin!
  Prince. Benvolio, who began this bloody fray? 155
  Benvolio. Tybalt here slain, whom Romeo's hand
    did slay.
Romeo that spoke him fair bid him bethink

140 **fool** dupe, plaything. 141 **Citizens** Q2 *Citti.* N. 143 **Citizen** Q2 *Citi.* SD all including the Prince's Train. 146 **discover** uncover, reveal. 147 **manage** conduct, proceeding. 151 **O husband** Q2 *O Cozen, husband;* for text see V.3.102 N. 157 **fair** civilly. **bethink** consider.

How nice the quarrel was and urg'd withal
Your high displeasure. All this uttered   159
With gentle breath, calm look, knees humbly bow'd,
Could not take truce with the unruly spleen
Of Tybalt, deaf to peace, but that he tilts
With piercing steel at bold Mercutio's breast,
Who all as hot turns deadly point to point
And with a martial scorn with one hand beats   165
Cold death aside and with the other sends
It back to Tybalt, whose dexterity
Retorts it. Romeo he cries aloud,
'Hold, friends! Friends, part!' and swifter than his
       tongue
His agile arm beats down their fatal points   170
And 'twixt them rushes; underneath whose arm
An envious thrust from Tybalt hit the life
Of stout Mercutio; and then Tybalt fled,
But by and by comes back to Romeo,
Who had but newly entertain'd revenge,   175
And to 't they go like lightning; for ere I
Could draw to part them was stout Tybalt slain,
And as he fell did Romeo turn and fly.
This is the truth or let Benvolio die.   179
    Capulet's Wife. He is a kinsman to the Montague,
Affection makes him false, he speaks not true.
Some twenty of them fought in this black strife,
And all those twenty could but kill one life.
I beg for justice, which thou, Prince, must give—
Romeo slew Tybalt, Romeo must not live.   185
    Prince. Romeo slew him, he slew Mercutio.

---

158 **nice** trivial. **withal** at the same time. 161 **take truce with** come
to terms with. **spleen** quarrelsomeness. 162 **tilts** thrusts. 165–6
one hand . . . the other N. 168 **Retorts** throws back. **Romeo he**
duplicated subject. 170 **agile** Q1; Q2 *aged*. 173 **stout** brave. 174 **by
and by** immediately. 175 **entertain'd** considered.

Who now the price of his dear blood doth owe?
  Montague. Not Romeo, Prince, he was Mercutio's
    friend.
His fault concludes but what the law should end—
The life of Tybalt.
  Prince.   And for that offence   190
Immediately we do exile him hence.
I have an int'rest in your hate's proceeding,
My blood for your rude brawls doth lie a-bleeding.
But I 'll amerce you with so strong a fine
That you shall all repent the loss of mine.   195
I will be deaf to pleading and excuses,
Nor tears nor prayers shall purchase out abuses.
Therefore use none. Let Romeo hence in haste,
Else when he 's found that hour is his last.
Bear hence this body and attend our will.   200
Mercy but murders, pardoning those that kill.
                                  Exeunt.

[SCENE 2]

Enter Juliet alone.

  Juliet. Gallop apace, you fiery-footed steeds,
Towards Phoebus' lodging. Such a wagoner
As Phaeton would whip you to the West
And bring in cloudy Night immediately.
Spread thy close curtain, love-performing Night,   5

187 **Who . . . owe** i.e. who now must pay for Tybalt's death.
188 **Montague** Q2 *Capu.* N. 191 **exile** here and elsewhere accented
'exíle.' 192 **hate's** Q1; Q2 *hearts.* 193 **My blood** since Mercutio
was the Prince's kinsman. 194 **amerce** punish by fine. 195 **mine**
i.e. my blood. 196 **I** Q1; Q2 *It.* 197 **purchase out** buy pardon for.
201 **Mercy . . . kill** N. 1–31 **Gallop apace . . . wear them** N. 1
steeds the horses of the sun god Phoebus Apollo. 3 **Phaeton** son
of Phoebus N.

That runaway's eyes may wink and Romeo
Leap to these arms untalk'd of and unseen.
Lovers can see to do their am'rous rites
By their own beauties, or if Love be blind
It best agrees with night. Come, civil Night,   10
Thou sober-suited matron all in black,
And learn me how to lose a winning match
Play'd for a pair of stainless maidenhoods.
Hood my unmann'd blood bating in my cheeks   14
With thy black mantle till strange love grow bold,
Think true love acted simple modesty.
Come Night, come Romeo, come thou day in night,
For thou wilt lie upon the wings of Night
Whiter than new snow upon a raven's back.   19
Come gentle Night, come loving black-brow'd Night,
Give me my Romeo. And when I shall die
Take him and cut him out in little stars,
And he will make the face of heav'n so fine
That all the world will be in love with Night
And pay no worship to the garish Sun.   25
O I have bought the mansion of a love
But not possess'd it, and though I am sold
Not yet enjoy'd. So tedious is this day
As is the night before some festival
To an impatient child that hath new robes   30
And may not wear them. O here comes my Nurse—

Enter Nurse with cords.

6 **runaway** i.e. the sun N. **wink** shut (i.e. cause darkness). 9 **By**
Q2 *And by;* for text see V.3.102 N. **Love** Cupid. 10 **civil** sober,
decorous. 14 **Hood** cover, blindfold (term from falconry). **unmann'd** untrained (of a falcon; quibble on 'without a man').
bating fluttering the wings. 17 **Night** pun on 'knight.' 25 **garish**
glaring. SD **Enter Nurse with cords** N. **cords** a rope ladder.

And she brings news, and every tongue that speaks
But Romeo's name speaks heav'nly eloquence.
Now Nurse, what news? What hast thou there,
The cords that Romeo bid thee fetch?

Nurse.   Ay, ay, the cords. 35

Juliet. Ay me, what news? why dost thou wring
      thy hands?

Nurse. Ah weraday, he's dead, he's dead, he's dead!
We are undone, lady, we are undone.
Alack the day! he's gone, he's kill'd, he's dead.

Juliet. Can Heaven be so envious?

Nurse.   Romeo can, 40
Though Heav'n cannot. O Romeo, Romeo!
Who ever would have thought it? Romeo!

Juliet. What divel art thou that dost torment me
      thus?
This torture should be roar'd in dismal Hell.
Hath Romeo slain himself? Say thou but 'Ay' 45
And that bare vowel 'I' shall poison more
Than the death-darting eye of cockatrice.
I am not I if there be such an 'Ay,'
Or those eyes shut that makes thee answer 'Ay.'
If he be slain say 'Ay' or if not 'No,' 50
Brief sounds determine my weal or woe.

Nurse. I saw the wound, I saw it with mine eyes
(God save the mark!) here on his manly breast.
A piteous corse, a bloody piteous corse,
Pale, pale as ashes, all bedaub'd in blood, 55
All in gore blood, I sounded at the sight.

37 **weraday** weladay, alas. 40 **envious** malicious. 46 **bare vowel 'I'**
the Elizabethan spelling of 'ay.' 47, 48 **eye, I** puns on 'ay.' 47
cockatrice basilisk N. 49 **those** Romeo's. 49 **shut** Q2 *shot.* 51 **determine** decide. 53 **God save the mark** God forbid. 54 **corse** corpse.
56 **gore** a clot of. **sounded** swounded, swooned.

71

Juliet. O break, my heart! poor bankrout, break at
  once!
To prison, eyes, ne'er look on liberty.
Vile earth to earth resign, end motion here,
And thou and Romeo press one heavy bier.   60
Nurse. O Tybalt, Tybalt, the best friend I had!
O courteous Tybalt, honest gentleman,
That ever I should live to see thee dead!
Juliet. What storm is this that blows so contrary?
Is Romeo slaughter'd and is Tybalt dead?   65
My dearest cousin and my dearer lord?
Then dreadful trumpet sound the general doom,
For who is living if those two are gone?
Nurse. Tybalt is gone and Romeo banished,
Romeo that kill'd him, he is banished.   70
Juliet. O God! did Romeo's hand shed Tybalt's
  blood?
Nurse. It did, it did! alas the day, it did!
Juliet. O serpent heart, hid with a flow'ring face!
Did ever dragon keep so fair a cave?
Beautiful tyrant, fiend angelical!   75
Dove-feather'd raven, wolvish-rav'ning lamb!
Despised substance of divinest show!
Just opposite to what thou justly seem'st,
A damned saint, an honorable villain!
O Nature, what hadst thou to do in Hell   80
When thou didst bow'r the spirit of a fiend

57 **bankrout** bankrupt. **break** quibble on 'declare insolvent.' 59
Vile earth wretched body. **resign** yield thyself up to. 67 **general
doom** Day of Judgment. 73–9 **O serpent heart . . . villain** see
I.1.179–84 N. 74 **keep** guard. **cave** i.e. containing treasure. 75
tyrant desperado, villain. 76 **Dove-feather'd** Q2 *Rauenous doue-
featherd;* for text see V.3.102 N. 77 **substance** reality. **show**
appearance. 78 **justly** truly. 79 **damned** Q2 *dimme.* 81 **bow'r**
*l*odge.

In mortal Paradise of such sweet flesh?
Was ever book containing such vile matter
So fairly bound? O that deceit should dwell
In such a gorgeous palace!   85
  Nurse. There 's no trust, no faith, no honesty in
     men,
All perjur'd, all forsworn, all dissemblers.
Ah, where 's my man? Give me some *aqua vitae*,
These griefs, these woes, these sorrows make me old.
Shame come to Romeo.
  Juliet.   Blister'd be thy tongue   90
For such a wish! He was not born to shame,
Upon his brow Shame is asham'd to sit,
For 'tis a throne where Honor may be crown'd
Sole monarch of the universal earth.
O what a beast was I to chide at him!   95
  Nurse. Will you speak well of him that kill'd your
     cousin?
  Juliet. Shall I speak ill of him that is my husband?
Ah poor my lord, what tongue shall smooth thy name
When I thy three-hours wife have mangled it?   99
But wherefore villain, didst thou kill my cousin?
That villain-cousin would have kill'd my husband.
Back, foolish tears, back to your native spring,
Your tributary drops belong to Woe,
Which you mistaking offer up to Joy.   104
My husband lives that Tybalt would have slain,
And Tybalt 's dead that would have slain my hus-
     band.
All this is comfort, wherefore weep I then?
Some word there was, worser than Tybalt's death,
That murder'd me. I would forget it fain,
But O it presses to my memory   110

87 forsworn, all Q2 *forsworne, all naught, all* N. 88 **aqua vitae**
spirits. 98 **smooth** speak well of (antithetic to *mangled*).

Like damned guilty deeds to sinners' minds:
'Tybalt is dead and Romeo banished.'
That 'banished,' that one word 'banished,'
Hath slain ten thousand Tybalts. Tybalt's death
Was woe enough if it had ended there,   115
Or if sour Woe delights in fellowship
And needly will be rank'd with other Griefs,
Why follow'd not (when she said 'Tybalt 's dead')
'Thy father' or 'Thy mother,' nay, or both,
Which modern lamentation might have mov'd?   120
But with a rear-ward following Tybalt's death,
'Romeo is banished'—to speak that word
Is father, mother, Tybalt, Romeo, Juliet,
All slain, all dead. 'Romeo is banished!'
There is no end, no limit, measure, bound,   125
In that word's death, no words can that woe sound.
Where is my father and my mother, Nurse?
   Nurse. Weeping and wailing over Tybalt's corse.
Will you go to them? I will bring you thither.
   Juliet. Wash they his wounds with tears? Mine shall
     be spent,   130
When theirs are dry, for Romeo's banishment.
Take up those cords. Poor ropes, you are beguil'd
(Both you and I) for Romeo is exil'd.
He made you for a highway to my bed,
But I a maid die maiden-widowed.   135
Come cords, come Nurse. I 'll to my wedding bed,
And Death, not Romeo, take my maidenhead!
   Nurse. Hie to your chamber, I 'll find Romeo
To comfort you, I wot well where he is.
Hark ye, your Romeo will be here at night.   140

---

117 **needly** of necessity. 120 **modern** ordinary. 121 **rear-ward** rear
guard. 126 **sound** utter, express (quibble on 'fathom'). 130 **spent**
shed. 139 **wot** know.

I 'll to him, he is hid at Lawrence' cell.

Juliet. O find him! Give this ring to my true knight
And bid him come to take his last farewell.   *Exeunt.*

[SCENE 3]

Enter Friar.

Friar. Romeo, come forth! come forth, thou fearful
    man.
Affliction is enamor'd of thy parts
And thou art wedded to Calamity.

⟨*Enter Romeo.*⟩

Romeo. Father, what news? what is the Prince's
    doom?
What Sorrow craves acquaintance at my hand   5
That I yet know not?
Friar.   Too familiar
Is my dear son with such sour company.
I bring thee tidings of the Prince's doom.
Romeo. What less than doomsday is the Prince's
    doom?   9
Friar. A gentler judgment vanish'd from his lips,
Not body's death but body's banishment.
Romeo. Ha! banishment! Be merciful, say 'death,'
For exile hath more terror in his look,
Much more, than death. Do not say 'banishment.'
Friar. Here from Verona art thou banished.   15
Be patient, for the world is broad and wide.
Romeo. There is no world without Verona walls,

SD **Enter Friar** So Q1; Q2 *Enter Frier and Romeo* N. 2 **parts**
qualities, endowments. 4 **doom** judgment. 6 **familiar** here pronounced 'famili-ar'; see I.4.94 N. 10 **vanish'd** was breathed,
issued. 17 **without** outside.

But Purgatory, torture, Hell itself.
Hence banished is banish'd from the world,
And world's exile is death. Then 'banished'   20
Is death misterm'd. Calling death 'banished'
Thou cut'st my head off with a golden ax
And smil'st upon the stroke that murders me.

   Friar. O deadly sin! O rude unthankfulness!   24
Thy fault our law calls death, but the kind Prince,
Taking thy part, hath rush'd aside the law
And turn'd that black word 'death' to 'banishment.'
This is dear mercy and thou see'st it not.

   Romeo. 'Tis torture and not mercy. Heav'n is here
Where Juliet lives, and every cat and dog   30
And little mouse, every unworthy thing,
Live here in Heaven and may look on her,
But Romeo may not. More validity,
More honorable state, more courtship lives
In carrion flies than Romeo—they may seize   35
On the white wonder of dear Juliet's hand
And steal immortal blessing from her lips,
Who e'en in pure and vestal modesty
Still blush, as thinking their own kisses sin,
But Romeo may not, he is banished.   40
Flies may do this but I from this must fly,
They are free men but I am banished.
And say'st thou yet that exile is not death?
Hadst thou no poison mix'd, no sharp-ground knife,
No sudden mean of death, though ne'er so mean,   45
But 'banished' to kill me? 'Banished!'
O Friar, the damned use that word in Hell,
Howling attends it. How hast thou the heart,

20 **world's** from this world. 26 **rush'd** thrust. 28 **dear** rare, unusual. 33 **validity** value. 34 **courtship** courtliness (quibble on 'wooing'). 40–3 **But Romeo . . . death** for text see II.1.230–3 N. 45 **mean** means. **so mean** so base.

Being a divine, a ghostly confessor,
A sin-absolver and my friend profess'd,   50
To mangle me with that word 'banished'?
  Friar. Thou fond mad man, hear me a little speak.
  Romeo. O thou wilt speak again of banishment.
  Friar. I 'll give thee armor to keep off that word,
Adversity's sweet milk, Philosophy,   55
To comfort thee though thou art banished.
  Romeo. Yet 'banished'? Hang up philosophy!
Unless philosophy can make a Juliet,
Displant a town, reverse a prince's doom,
It helps not, it prevails not. Talk no more.   60
  Friar. O then I see that mad men have no ears.
  Romeo. How should they, when that wise men have
    no eyes?
  Friar. Let me dispute with thee of thy estate.
  Romeo. Thou canst not speak of that thou dost not
    feel.
Wert thou as young as I, Juliet thy love,   65
An hour but marry'd, Tybalt murdered,
Doting like me and like me banished,
Then mightst thou speak—then mightst thou tear
    thy hair
And fall upon the ground as I do now,
Taking the measure of an unmade grave.   70
          ⟨*Nurse knocks* [*within.*]⟩
  Friar. Arise, one knocks! good Romeo, hide thyself.
  Romeo. Not I, unless the breath of heartsick groans
Mistlike infold me from the search of eyes.
               ⟨*She knocks again.*⟩

49 confessor stressed ´ – ´. **52 Thou** Q1; Q2 *Then*. **fond** foolish.
57 Yet still. **59 Displant** uproot. **60 prevails** avails. **63 dispute**
discuss. **estate** situation. **64 that** that which. SD ⟨**Nurse knocks**⟩
Q2 *Enter Nurse, and knocke*. SD ⟨**She knocks again**⟩ Q2 *They
knock*.

Friar. Hark! how they knock. Who's there? Romeo,
    arise,
Thou wilt be taken. Stay a while! Stand up.   75
                              Loud knock.
Run to my study— By and by! God's will,
What simpleness is this? I come, I come!   *Knock.*
Who knocks so hard? whence come you? what's your
    will?

Enter Nurse.

Nurse. Let me come in and you shall know my
    errand.
I come from Lady Juliet.
  Friar.   Welcome then.   80
  Nurse. O holy Friar, O tell me, holy Friar,
Where is my lady's lord, where's Romeo?
  Friar. There on the ground, with his own tears
    made drunk.
  Nurse. O he is even in my mistress' case,
Just in her case! O woeful sympathy,   85
Piteous predicament—e'en so lies she
Blubb'ring and weeping, weeping and blubb'ring.
Stand up, stand up! stand and you be a man,
For Juliet's sake, for her sake, rise and stand.   89
Why should you fall into so deep an O?   ⟨*He rises.*⟩
  Romeo. Nurse—
  Nurse.   Ah sir! ah sir! death's the end of all.
  Romeo. Spak'st thou of Juliet? how is it with her?
Doth not she think me an old murtherer
Now I have stain'd the childhood of our joy

SD **Loud knock** Q2 *Slud knock.* 76 **By and by** immediately.
77 **simpleness** folly. 84 **case** quibble on 'pudendum.' 85 **woeful
sympathy** agreement in woe. 87 **Blubb'ring** weeping hard. 88
and if. 90 **O** moan, lament (quibble on 'pudendum'; compare
II.1.24). 93 **old** experienced, hardened.

With blood remov'd but little from her own? 95
Where is she? and how doth she? and what says
My conceal'd lady to our cancel'd love?
   Nurse. O she says nothing, sir, but weeps and weeps,
And now falls on her bed and then starts up,
And Tybalt calls and then on Romeo cries 100
And then down falls again.
   Romeo.   As if that name
Shot from the deadly level of a gun
Did murther her, as that name's cursed hand
Murder'd her kinsman. O tell me, Friar, tell me,
In what vile part of this anatomy 105
Doth my name lodge? tell me, that I may sack
The hateful mansion.
   ⟨*He offers to stab himself, and Nurse snatches
the dagger away.*⟩
   Friar.   Hold thy desp'rate hand!
Art thou a man? thy form cries out thou art—
Thy tears are wom'nish, thy wild acts denote
Th' unreasonable fury of a beast. 110
Unseemly woman in a seeming man,
And ill-beseeming beast in seeming both,
Thou hast amaz'd me. By my holy order,
I thought thy disposition better temper'd. 114
Hast thou slain Tybalt? wilt thou slay thyself?
And slay thy lady that in thy life lives
By doing damned hate upon thyself?
Why rail'st thou on thy birth, the Heav'n and earth?
Since birth and Heav'n and earth all three do meet

97 **conceal'd** secret (since the marriage is not known; stressed
⁻ ⁻ to jingle with *cancel'd*). 102 **level** line of aim. 105 **anatomy**
body. SD **Nurse** in the modern theater usually the Friar. 114
temper'd mixed, balanced. 116 **lives** Q1; Q2 *lies*. 117 **damned**
since suicide is an unforgivable sin.

In thee at once, which thou at once wouldst lose.
Fie, fie! thou sham'st thy shape, thy love, thy wit,
Which like a usurer abound'st in all
And usest none in that true use indeed
Which should bedeck thy shape, thy love, thy wit.
Thy noble shape is but a form of wax   125
Digressing from the valor of a man;
Thy dear love sworn, but hollow perjury,
Killing that love which thou hast vow'd to cherish;
Thy wit (that ornament to shape and love,
Misshapen in the conduct of them both)   130
Like powder in a skill-less soldier's flask
Is set afire by thine own ignorance,
And thou dismember'd with thine own defence.
What! rouse thee, man, thy Juliet is alive,   134
For whose dear sake thou wast but lately dead—
There art thou happy. Tybalt would kill thee,
But thou slew'st Tybalt—there art thou happy.
The law that threaten'd death becomes thy friend
And turns it to exile—there art thou happy.
A pack of blessings light upon thy back,   140
Happiness courts thee in her best array,
But like a misbehav'd and sullen wench
Thou pouts upon thy fortune and thy love.
Take heed, take heed, for such die mis'rable.
Go get thee to thy love as was decree'd,   145
Ascend her chamber, hence and comfort her.
But look thou stay not till the watch be set,
For then thou canst not pass to Mantua,

121 wit judgment, reason. 122 Which who. 123 usest quibble on
'lend at interest.' 126 Digressing deviating. 136 There in that
respect. 143 pouts upon Q2 *puts vp;* Q1 *frownst vpon.* 145 decree'd
arranged. 147 watch guard. set posted (at the city gates).

Where thou shalt live till we can find a time
To blaze your marriage, reconcile your friends,
Beg pardon of the Prince and call thee back   151
With twenty hundred thousand times more joy
Than thou went'st forth in lamentation.
Go before, Nurse, commend me to thy lady,
And bid her hasten all the house to bed,   155
Which heavy sorrow makes them apt unto.
Romeo is coming.
  Nurse. O Lord, I could have stay'd here all the
    night
To hear good counsel, O what learning is!
My lord, I 'll tell my lady you will come.   160
  Romeo. Do so, and bid my sweet prepare to chide.
    ⟨*Nurse offers to go in and turns again.*⟩
  Nurse. Here sir, a ring she bid me give you, sir.
Hie you, make haste, for it grows very late.
  Romeo. How well my comfort is reviv'd by this!
  Friar. Go hence, good night.   ⟨*Exit Nurse.*⟩
            And here stands all your state: 165
Either be gone before the watch be set
Or by the break of day disguis'd from hence.
Sojourn in Mantua. I'll find out your man,
And he shall signify from time to time
Every good hap to you that chances here.   170
Give me thy hand, 'tis late. Farewell, good night.
  Romeo. But that a joy past joy calls out on me,
It were a grief so brief to part with thee.
Farewell.   *Exeunt.*

150 **blaze** proclaim. **friends** relatives, families. 156 **apt** inclined.
SD **again** back. 165 **here . . . state** here is the situation. 166–7
Either be gone . . . hence N. 172 **But that** were it not that.
173 **were** would be. **brief** hastily.

81

[SCENE 4]

Enter old Capulet, his Wife and Paris.

Capulet. Things have fall'n out, sir, so unluckily
That we have had no time to move our daughter.
Look you, she lov'd her kinsman Tybalt dearly,
And so did I. Well, we were born to die.
'Tis very late, she 'll not come down tonight.   5
I promise you, but for your company
I would have been abed an hour ago.
Paris. These times of woe afford no times to woo.
Madam, good night, commend me to your daughter.
Wife. I will, and know her mind early tomorrow.
Tonight she 's mew'd up to her heaviness.   11
⟨*Paris offers to go in, and Capulet calls him again.*⟩
Capulet. Sir Paris, I will make a desp'rate tender
Of my child's love. I think she will be rul'd
In all respects by me; nay more, I doubt it not.
Wife, go you to her ere you go to bed,   15
Acquaint her here of my son Paris' love
And bid her (mark you me?) on Wednesday next—
But soft, what day is this?
Paris.   Monday, my lord.
Capulet. Monday. Ha, ha! Well, Wednesday is too
          soon.
A Thursday let it be—a Thursday, tell her,   20
She shall be marry'd to this noble earl.
Will you be ready? do you like this haste?
We 'll keep no great ado—a friend or two—

2 **move** urge, persuade. 6 **promise** assure. 11 **mew'd up** to shut up
with (a 'mew' being a falcon's cage). **heaviness** sorrow. SD **again**
back. 12 **desp'rate tender** reckless offer N. 16 **son** intended son-in-
law. 20 **A** on. 21 **earl** nobleman, count.

82

For hark you, Tybalt being slain so late,
It may be thought we held him carelessly,   25
Being our kinsman, if we revel much.
Therefore we 'll have some half a dozen friends
And there an end. But what say you to Thursday?
  Paris. My lord, I would that Thursday were to-
     morrow.   29
  Capulet. Well, get you gone, a Thursday be it then.
Go you to Juliet ere you go to bed,
Prepare her, Wife, against this wedding day.
Farewell, my lord. Light to my chamber, ho!
Afore me, it is so very late
That we may call it early by and by.   35
Good night.   *Exeunt.*

[SCENE 5]

Enter Romeo and Juliet ⟨at the window⟩.

  Juliet. Wilt thou be gone? it is not yet near day,
It was the nightingale and not the lark
That pierc'd the fearful hollow of thine ear,
Nightly she sings on yond pomegranate tree.
Believe me, love, it was the nightingale.   5
  Romeo. It was the lark, the herald of the morn,
No nightingale. Look love, what envious streaks
Do lace the sev'ring clouds in yonder East—
Night's candles are burnt out and jocund Day
Stands tiptoe on the misty mountain tops.   10
I must be gone and live or stay and die.
  Juliet. Yond light is not daylight, I know it, I.

32 against in readiness for. 34 Afore me on my word (a mild oath).
SD ⟨at the window⟩ Q2 *aloft.* 1–36 Wilt thou be gone . . . **dark
our woes** N. 3 fearful apprehensive. 7 envious malicious. 8 lace
streak.

It is some meteor that the sun exhal'd
To be to thee this night a torchbearer
And light thee on thy way to Mantua.   15
Therefore stay yet, thou need'st not to be gone.

   Romeo. Let me be tane, let me be put to death,
I am content, so thou wilt have it so.
I 'll say yon grey is not the Morning's eye—
'Tis but the pale reflex of Cynthia's brow;   20
Nor that is not the lark whose notes do beat
The vaulty heav'n so high above our heads.
I have more care to stay than will to go.
Come death, and welcome! Juliet wills it so.
How is 't, my soul? let 's talk, it is not day.   25

   Juliet. It is, it is! hie hence, be gone away.
It is the lark that sings so out of tune,
Straining harsh discords and unpleasing sharps.
Some say the lark makes sweet division,
This doth not so for she divideth us.   30
Some say the lark and loathed toad chang'd eyes,
O now I would they had chang'd voices too,
Since arm from arm that voice doth us affray,
Hunting thee hence with hunt's-up to the day.
O now be gone, more light and light it grows.   35

   Romeo. More light and light—more dark and dark
     our woes.

Enter Nurse ⟨hastily⟩.

13 **meteor** supposedly the ignition of vapors exhaled from the
earth. **exhal'd** Q2 *exhale;* Q1 *exhales;* drew up N. 17 **tane** taken.
18 **so** if. 20 **reflex** reflected light. **Cynthia** the moon. 23 **care**
concern, desire. 28 **sharps** shrill high notes. 29 **division** modula-
tion, melody. 31 **Some say . . . eyes** N. **chang'd** Q2 *change;* ex-
changed. 33 **arm from arm** from one another's arms. **affray** startle.
34 **hunt's-up** morning song (to waken hunters or a new-married
wife). **SD Nurse** so Q1; Q2 *Madame and Nurse* N.

Nurse. Madam!

Juliet. Nurse?

Nurse. Your lady mother 's coming to your chamber.   39

The day is broke, be wary, look about.   [*Exit.*]

Juliet. Then window, let day in and let life out.

Romeo. Farewell, farewell! one kiss, and I 'll descend.   ⟨*He goeth down.*⟩

Juliet. Art thou gone so, love? Lord, my husband, friend,

I must hear from thee every day i' th' hour,

For in a minute there are many days—   45

O by this count I shall be much in years

Ere I again behold my Romeo.

Romeo. Farewell.

I will omit no opportunity

That may convey my greetings, love, to thee.   50

Juliet. O think'st thou we shall ever meet again?

Romeo. Ay, doubt it not, and all these woes shall serve

For sweet discourses in our times to come.

Juliet. O God! I have an ill-divining soul,

Methinks I see thee, now thou art so low,   55

As one dead in the bottom of a tomb.

Either my eyesight fails or thou look'st pale.

Romeo. And trust me, love, in my eye so do you—

Dry Sorrow drinks our blood. Adieu, adieu!   *Exit.*

Juliet. O Fortune, Fortune! all men call thee fickle.

If thou art fickle, what dost thou with him   61

That is renowm'd for faith? Be fickle, Fortune,

37–40 **Madam . . . look about** for staging see N. 41 **life** i.e.
Romeo. 43 **my** Q1; Q2 *ay.* **friend** lover. 46 **count** method of
reckoning time. 52 **Ay** Q2 *I* (usually here interpreted as the pronoun). 54 **ill-divining** prophesying mischance. 59 **Dry . . . blood**
since grief was thought to exhaust the blood. 62 **renowm'd** N.

For then I hope thou wilt not keep him long
But send him back—

Enter Capulet's Wife.

Wife.   Ho daughter! are you up?
Juliet. Who is 't that calls? it is my lady mother,
Is she not down so late or up so early?   66
What unaccustom'd cause procures her hither?
                    ⟨*She goeth down from the window.*⟩
Wife. Why how now, Juliet?
Juliet.   Madam I am not well.
Wife. Evermore weeping for your cousin's death?
What! wilt thou wash him from his grave with tears?
And if thou couldst, thou couldst not make him live,
Therefore have done. Some grief shows much of love,
But much of grief shows still some want of wit.
Juliet. Yet let me weep for such a feeling loss.   74
Wife. So shall you feel the loss, but not the friend
Which you weep for.
Juliet.   Feeling so the loss,
I cannot choose but ever weep the friend.
Wife. Well girl, thou weep'st not so much for his
     death
As that the villain lives which slaughter'd him.   79
Juliet. What villain, madam?
Wife.   That same villain Romeo.
Juliet. [*Aside.*] 'Villain' and he be many miles
     asunder.
God pardon him, I do with all my heart,
And yet no man like he doth grieve my heart.
Wife. That is because the traitor murd'rer lives.

66 **down** lying down, abed. 67 **procures** brings. SD ⟨She . . .
window⟩ for staging see N. 74 **feeling** heartfelt. 76 **Which** whom.
82 **him** Q2 omits. 83 **like** so much as.
86

Juliet. Ay madam, from the reach of these my
    hands,   85
Would none but I might venge my cousin's death!
  Wife. We will have vengeance for it, fear thou not.
Then weep no more, I 'll send to one in Mantua,
Where that same banish'd runagate doth live.
Shall give him such an unaccustom'd dram   90
That he shall soon keep Tybalt company,
And then I hope thou wilt be satisfy'd.
  Juliet. Indeed I never shall be satisfy'd
With Romeo till I behold him—dead—
Is my poor heart so for a kinsman vex'd.   95
Madam, if you could find out but a man
To bear a poison, I would temper it
That Romeo should upon receipt thereof
Soon sleep in quiet. O how my heart abhors
To hear him nam'd and cannot come to him   100
To wreak the love I bore my cousin
Upon his body that hath slaughter'd him.
  Wife. Find thou the means and I'll find such a man.
But now I 'll tell thee joyful tidings, girl.   104
  Juliet. And joy comes well in such a needy time.
What are they, I beseech your ladyship?
  Wife. Well, well, thou hast a careful father, child,
One who to put thee from thy heaviness
Hath sorted out a sudden day of joy
That thou expects not nor I look'd not for.   110
  Juliet. Madam, in happy time, what day is that?
  Wife. Marry, my child, early next Thursday morn

89 **runagate** renegade, fugitive. 90 **Shall** who shall. 94 **dead** to be
construed with both *him* and *heart*. 97 **temper** mix (quibble on
'mitigate'). 98 **That** so that. 101 **wreak** avenge (quibble on
'express'). 106 **I** Q2 omits. 107 **careful** provident. 109 **sorted out**
arranged for. 110 **nor I look'd not for** intensifying double negative. 111 **in happy time** how opportune.

The gallant, young and noble gentleman,
The County Paris, at Saint Peter's Church
Shall happily make thee there a joyful bride. 115
  Juliet. Now by Saint Peter's Church and Peter too,
He shall not make me there a joyful bride.
I wonder at this haste, that I must wed
Ere he that should be husband comes to woo.
I pray you tell my lord and father, madam, 120
I will not marry yet, and when I do, I swear
It shall be Romeo, whom you know I hate,
Rather than Paris. These are news indeed!
  Wife. Here comes your father, tell him so yourself,
And see how he will take it at your hands. 125

Enter Capulet and Nurse.

  Capulet. When the sun sets the earth doth drizzle
    dew,
But for the sunset of my brother's son
It rains downright.
How now, a conduit, girl? what! still in tears?
Evermore showering? In one little body 130
Thou counterfeits a bark, a sea, a wind:
For still thy eyes, which I may call the sea,
Do ebb and flow with tears; the bark thy body is,
Sailing in this salt flood; the winds, thy sighs,
Who, raging with thy tears and they with them, 135
Without a sudden calm will overset
Thy tempest-tossed body. How now, Wife,
Have you deliver'd to her our decree?
  Wife. Ay sir, but she will none, she gives you
    thanks,

127 **brother** brother-in-law. 129 **conduit** fountain (sometimes
made in the shape of a human figure). 135 **Who** which. 139 **will
none** will have none of it.
88

I would the fool were marry'd to her grave.   140

  Capulet. Soft! take me with you, take me with you,
     Wife.

How! will she none? doth she not give us thanks?

Is she not proud? doth she not count her blest,

Unworthy as she is, that we have wrought

So worthy a gentleman to be her bride?   145

  Juliet. Not proud you have, but thankful that you
     have.

Proud can I never be of what I hate,

But thankful e'en for hate that is meant love.

  Capulet. How, how, how, how, chopt-logic? What
     is this?

'Proud' and 'I thank you' and 'I thank you not'   150

And yet 'not proud'? Mistress minion you,

Thank me no thankings nor proud me no prouds,

But fettle your fine joints 'gainst Thursday next

To go with Paris to Saint Peter's Church,

Or I will drag thee on a hurdle thither.   155

Out! you green-sickness carrion, out! you baggage,

You tallow-face!

  Wife.   Fie, fie—what! are you mad?

  Juliet. Good father, I beseech you on my knees,
                ⟨*She kneels down.*⟩

Hear me with patience but to speak a word.

  Capulet. Hang thee! young baggage, disobedient
     wretch!   160

I tell thee what, get thee to church a Thursday

Or never after look me in the face.

141 **take me with you** let me understand you. 144 **wrought** arranged for. 145 **bride** bridegroom. 149 **chopt-logic** sophistical argument. 151 **minion** hussy. 153 **fettle** make ready. **'gainst** in preparation for. 155 **hurdle** a sledge for dragging traitors to execution. 156 **green-sickness** anemia affecting adolescent girls. **carrion** lump of flesh. 157 **tallow** i.e. yellowish-white.

Speak not, reply not, do not answer me!
My fingers itch. Wife, we scarce thought us blest
That God had lent us but this only child,   165
But now I see this one is one too much
And that we have a curse in having her.
Out on her, hilding!

Nurse.   God in Heaven bless her!
You are to blame, my lord, to rate her so.

Capulet. And why, my Lady Wisdom? Hold your
tongue,   170
Good Prudence; smatter with your gossips, go!

Nurse. I speak no treason.

Capulet.   O—Godigoden!

Nurse. May not one speak?

Capulet.   Peace! you mumbling fool.
Utter your gravity o'er a goship's bowl,
For here we need it not.

Wife.   You are too hot.   175

Capulet. God's bread! it makes me mad. Day,
night—work, play—
Alone, in company—still my care hath been
To have her match'd; and having now provided
A gentleman of noble parentage,
Of fair demesnes, youthful and nobly limb'd,   180
Stuff'd, as they say, with honorable parts,
Proportion'd as one's thought would wish a man—
And then to have a wretched puling fool,

---

168 **hilding** baggage. 169 **rate** berate; see III.4.12 N. 171 **smatter** prate. 172, 173 **Capulet, Nurse** N. 172 **Godigoden** God give ye good e'en. 174 **goship** gossip (originally a godparent or sponsor at a baptism). **bowl** christening cup. 176 **God's bread** the Host (the consecrated bread of the Eucharist). **Day, night—work, play** N. 180 **demesnes** domains, landed property. **limb'd** Q2 *liand;* Q1 *trainde* N. 181 **parts** qualities. 183 **puling** whimpering.

A whining mammet, in her fortune's tender
To answer 'I 'll not wed, I cannot love,   185
I am too young, I pray you pardon me!'
But and you will not wed I 'll pardon you—
Graze where you will, you shall not house with me.
Look to 't, think on 't, I do not use to jest.
Thursday is near, lay hand on heart, advise.   190
And you be mine, I 'll give you to my friend,
And you be not, hang, beg, starve, die in the streets,
For by my soul I 'll ne'er acknowledge thee
Nor what is mine shall never do thee good.   194
Trust to 't, bethink you, I 'll not be forsworn.   *Exit.*
  Juliet. Is there no Pity sitting in the clouds
That sees into the bottom of my grief?
O sweet my mother, cast me not away,
Delay this marriage for a month, a week,
Or if you do not, make the bridal bed   200
In that dim monument where Tybalt lies.
  Wife. Talk not to me, for I 'll not speak a word,
Do as thou wilt, for I have done with thee.   *Exit.*
  Juliet. O God! O Nurse, how shall this be pre-
      vented?
My husband is on earth, my faith in Heaven.   205
How shall that faith return again to earth
Unless that husband send it me from Heaven
By leaving earth? Comfort me, counsel me!
Alack, alack, that Heav'n should practice stratagems
Upon so soft a subject as myself!   210
What say'st thou? hast thou not a word of joy?

184 **mammet** doll, puppet (from 'Mahomet,' thought of as an
idol). **in her fortune's tender** on the offer of good fortune. 187
pardon you quibble on 'give leave to depart.' 189 **do not use**
am not accustomed. 190 **advise** be advised, consider. 195 **be
forsworn** break my oath. 201 **monument** burial vault. 205 **faith**
marriage vow. 209 **stratagems** dreadful deeds.

Some comfort, Nurse.

  Nurse.   Faith, here it is:

Romeo is banish'd, and all the world to nothing

That he dares ne'er come back to challenge you,

Or if he do it needs must be by stealth.   215

Then since the case so stands as now it doth,

I think it best you marry'd with the County.

O he 's a lovely gentleman!

Romeo 's a dishclout to him. An eagle, madam,

Hath not so green, so quick, so fair an eye   220

As Paris hath. Beshrew my very heart,

I think you 're happy in this second match,

For it excels your first, or if 't did not

Your first is dead—or 'twere as good he were,

As living here and you no use of him.   225

  Juliet. Speak'st thou from thy heart?

  Nurse. And from my soul too, else beshrew them
    both.

  Juliet. Amen.

  Nurse. What?

  Juliet. Well, thou hast comforted me marvelous
    much.   230

Go in and tell my lady I am gone,

Having displeas'd my father, to Lawrence' cell

To make confession and to be absolv'd.

  Nurse. Marry I will, and this is wisely done. [*Exit.*]

                ⟨*Juliet looks after Nurse.*⟩

  Juliet. Ancient damnation! O most wicked fiend!

---

213 **all the world to nothing** i.e. the odds are very great. 214
challenge claim. 219 **dishclout** dishcloth. **to** in comparison to.
220 **green** a color much admired in eyes. **quick** lively. 221 **Beshrew**
curse. 225 **here** i.e. in this world. SD ⟨Juliet⟩ Q1 *She.* 235 **Ancient
damnation** damned old woman.

Is it more sin to wish me thus forsworn,   236
Or to dispraise my lord with that same tongue
Which she hath prais'd him with above compare
So many thousand times? Go counselor,
Thou and my bosom henceforth shall be twain.   240
I 'll to the Friar to know his remedy,
If all else fail, myself have power to die.   *Exit.*

236 forsworn i.e. by breaking the marriage vow.

Enter Friar and County Paris.

Friar. On Thursday, sir? the time is very short.
Paris. My father Capulet will have it so,
And I am nothing slow to slack his haste.
Friar. You say you do not know the lady's mind?
Uneven is the course, I like it not.   5
Paris. Immoderately she weeps for Tybalt's death,
And therefore have I little talk'd of love,
For Venus smiles not in a house of tears.
Now sir, her father counts it dangerous
That she do give her sorrow so much sway,   10
And in his wisdom hastes our marriage
To stop the inundation of her tears,
Which, too much minded by herself alone,
May be put from her by society.
Now do you know the reason of this haste.   15
   Friar. [*Aside.*] I would I knew not why it should
        be slow'd!
Look sir, here comes the lady toward my cell.

Enter Juliet.

Paris. Happily met, my lady and my wife.
Juliet. That may be, sir, when I may be a wife.

2 **father** intended father-in-law. 3 **nothing slow** extremely re-
luctant (intensifying double negative). 5 **Uneven** irregular. 7
talk'd Q2 *talke.*

Paris. That 'may be' must be, love, on Thursday
    next.   20
Juliet. What must be shall be.
Friar.   That 's a certain text.
Paris. Come you to make confession to this Father?
Juliet. To answer that, I should confess to you.
Paris. Do not deny to him that you love me.
Juliet. I will confess to you that I love him.   25
Paris. So will ye, I am sure, that you love me.
Juliet. If I do so, it will be of more price
Being spoke behind your back than to your face.
Paris. Poor soul, thy face is much abus'd with
    tears.   29
Juliet. The tears have got small victory by that,
For it was bad enough before their spite.
Paris. Thou wrong'st it more than tears with that
    report.
Juliet. That is no slander, sir, which is a truth,
And what I spake, I spake it to my face.   34
Paris. Thy face is mine, and thou hast slander'd it.
Juliet. It may be so, for it is not mine own.
Are you at leisure, holy Father, now,
Or shall I come to you at evening mass?
Friar. My leisure serves me, pensive daughter, now.
My lord, we must entreat the time alone.   40
Paris. God shield I should disturb devotion.
Juliet, on Thursday early will I rouse ye.
Till then, adieu, and keep this holy kiss.   *Exit.*
Juliet. O shut the door! and when thou hast done so,
Come weep with me—past hope, past cure, past help.
Friar. O Juliet, I already know thy grief,   46

27 **price** value. 29 **abus'd** disfigured. 31 **spite** injury. 34 **to my face**
frankly (quibble on 'about my face'). 38 **evening mass** N. 39
pensive sorrowful. 40 **entreat** ask to have. 41 **shield** prevent,
forbid. 45 **cure** Q1; Q2 *care.*

It strains me past the compass of my wits.
I hear thou must, and nothing may prorogue it,
On Thursday next be marry'd to this County.   49
   Juliet. Tell me not, Friar, that thou hear'st of this,
Unless thou tell me how I may prevent it.
If in thy wisdom thou canst give no help,
Do thou but call my resolution wise
And with this knife I 'll help it presently.   54
God join'd my heart and Romeo's, thou our hands,
And ere this hand by thee to Romeo's seal'd
Shall be the label to another deed,
Or my true heart with treacherous revolt
Turn to another, this shall slay them both.
Therefore out of thy long-experienc'd time   60
Give me some present counsel, or behold
'Twixt my extremes and me this bloody knife
Shall play the umpeer, arbitrating that
Which the commission of thy years and art
Could to no issue of true honor bring.   65
Be not so long to speak, I long to die
If what thou speak'st speak not of remedy.
   Friar. Hold daughter, I do spy a kind of hope
Which craves as desperate an execution
As that is desp'rate which we would prevent.   70
If rather than to marry County Paris
Thou hast the strength of will to slay thyself,
Then is it likely thou wilt undertake
A thing like death to chide away this shame,   74
That cop'st with Death himself to scape from it,
And if thou dar'st I'll give thee remedy.

48 **prorogue** postpone. 57 **label** i.e. a wax seal N. **deed** quibble
on 'act.' 61 **present** immediate. 63 **umpeer** umpire N. 64 **commission** authority. 72 **slay** Q1; Q2 *stay.* 74 **chide** drive. 75 **cop'st**
wouldst negotiate.

Juliet. O bid me leap, rather than marry Paris,
From off the battlements of any tower
Or walk in thievish ways, or bid me lurk   79
Where serpents are; chain me with roaring bears,
Or hide me nightly in a charnel house,
O'ercover'd quite with dead men's rattling bones,
With reeky shanks and yellow chapless skulls;
Or bid me go into a new-made grave
And hide me with a dead man in his shroud—   85
Things that to hear them told have made me trem-
        ble—
And I will do it without fear or doubt
To live an unstain'd wife to my sweet love.
    Friar. Hold, then. Go home, be merry, give consent
To marry Paris. Wednesday is tomorrow.   90
Tomorrow night look that thou lie alone,
Let not the Nurse lie with thee in thy chamber.
Take thou this vial, being then in bed,
And this distilling liquor drink thou off,
When presently through all thy veins shall run   95
A cold and drowsy humor—for no pulse
Shall keep his native progress, but surcease;
No warmth, no breath shall testify thou livest;
The roses in thy lips and cheeks shall fade
To wanny ashes, thy eyes' windows fall   100
Like Death when he shuts up the day of life.
Each part, depriv'd of supple government,

79 **thievish** full of thieves. 81 **charnel house** bone vault N. 83
reeky rankly moist. **chapless** Q1; Q2 *chapels;* jawless. 85 **shroud**
Q2 omits. 88 **unstain'd** stressed $\acute{\ }$ $\ ^{-}$. 94 **distilling** distilled. 96
drowsy sleep inducing. **humor** fluid. 97 **native progress** natural
motion. **surcease** shall cease. 98 **breath** Q2 *breast.* 100 **wanny**
Q2 *many* N. 102 **supple government** the faculty of supple move-
ment.

Shall stiff and stark and cold appear like death,
And in this borrow'd likeness of shrunk death
Thou shalt continue two and forty hours   105
And then awake as from a pleasant sleep.
Now when the bridegroom in the morning comes
To rouse thee from thy bed, there art thou dead.
Then as the manner of our country is
In thy best robes uncover'd on the bier   110
Thou shall be borne to that same ancient vault
Where all the kindred of the Capulets lie.
In the meantime, against thou shalt awake,
Shall Romeo by my letters know our drift,
And hither shall he come; and he and I   115
Will watch thy waking, and that very night
Shall Romeo bear thee hence to Mantua.
And this shall free thee from this present shame
If no inconstant toy nor wom'nish fear
Abate thy valor in the acting it.   120

Juliet. Give me, give me! O tell not me of fear!

Friar. Hold, get you gone. Be strong and prosper-
ous
In this resolve. I 'll send a friar with speed
To Mantua with my letters to thy lord.

Juliet. Love give me strength! and strength shall
    help afford.   125
Farewell, dear Father.   *Exeunt.*

105 **two and forty hours** N. 110 **uncover'd** with face uncovered.
111–12 **Thou shall . . . lie** for text see II.1.230–3 N. 114 **letters**
letter. **drift** plot. 119 **toy** crotchet (i.e. unreasoning aversion).

[SCENE 2]

Enter Capulet, his Wife, Nurse and Servingmen,
two or three.

Capulet. So many guests invite as here are writ.
                              [*Exit a Servingman.*]
Sirrah, go hire me twenty cunning cooks.
  Servingman. You shall have none ill, sir, for I 'll
try if they can lick their fingers.
  Capulet. How canst thou try them so?   5
  Servingman. Marry sir, 'tis an ill cook that cannot
lick his own fingers; therefore he that cannot lick
his fingers goes not with me.
  Capulet. Go, be gone.

                              ⟨*Exit Servingman.*⟩
We shall be much unfurnish'd for this time.   10
What, is my daughter gone to Friar Lawrence?
  Nurse. Ay forsooth.
  Capulet. Well, he may chance to do some good on
      her,
A peevish self-will'd harlotry it is.

Enter Juliet.

  Nurse. See where she comes from shrift with merry
      look.   15
  Capulet. How now my headstrong, where have you
      been gadding?
  Juliet. Where I have learnt me to repent the sin
Of disobedient opposition

SD **Servingmen** see I.4.1 SD N. 2 **cunning** skillful. 10 **unfurnish'd**
unprovisioned. 14 **peevish** silly. **harlotry** wench. **it** she (used
affectionately).

To you and your behests, and am enjoin'd
By holy Lawrence to fall prostrate here   20
                         ⟨*She kneels down.*⟩
To beg your pardon. Pardon, I beseech you,
Henceforward I am ever rul'd by you.
  Capulet. Send for the County, go, tell him of this.
I 'll have this knot knit up tomorrow morning.   24
  Juliet. I met the youthful lord at Lawrence' cell
And gave him what becomed love I might,
Not stepping o'er the bounds of modesty.
  Capulet. Why, I am glad on 't, this is well. Stand
    up.
This is as 't should be. Let me see the County.
Ay marry, go, I say, and fetch him hither.   30
Now afore God, this reverend holy Friar,
All our whole city is much bound to him.
  Juliet. Nurse, will you go with me into my closet
To help me sort such needful ornaments
As you think fit to furnish me tomorrow?   35
  Wife. No, not till Thursday, there is time enough.
  Capulet. Go Nurse, go with her, we 'll to church
    tomorrow.
                         Exeunt ⟨*Nurse and Juliet*⟩.
  Wife. We shall be short in our provision,
'Tis now near night.
  Capulet.   Tush, I will stir about,   39
And all things shall be well, I warrant thee, Wife.
Go thou to Juliet, help to deck up her.
I 'll not to bed tonight, let me alone,
I 'll play the huswife for this once. What ho!

---

24 **knot** bond of wedlock. 26 **becomed** befitting. 32 **bound** indebted. 33 **closet** private room. 34 **sort** select. SD **Exeunt** ⟨Nurse
and Juliet⟩ for staging see N. 41 **up** completely. 43 **huswife** house-
wife, hussy (pronounced 'huzzif').

They are all forth. Well, I will walk myself
To County Paris, to prepare up him   45
Against tomorrow. My heart is wondrous light
Since this same wayward girl is so reclaim'd.
                                        Exeunt.

[SCENE 3]

Enter Juliet and Nurse.

Juliet. Ay those attires are best. But gentle Nurse,
I pray thee leave me to myself tonight,
For I have need of many orisons
To move the Heav'ns to smile upon my state,
Which well thou know'st is cross and full of sin.   5

Enter Capulet's Wife.

Wife. What, are you busy, ho? need you my help?
Juliet. No madam, we have cull'd such necessaries
As are behooful for our state tomorrow.
So please you, let me now be left alone,
And let the Nurse this night sit up with you,   10
For I am sure you have your hands full all
In this so sudden business.
 Wife.   Good night,
Get thee to bed and rest, for thou hast need.
                    Exeunt [Wife and Nurse].
Juliet. Farewell! God knows when we shall meet
        again.   14
I have a faint cold fear thrills through my veins
That almost freezes up the heat of life.

3 **orisons** prayers. 4 **state** condition. 5 **cross** contrary. 8 **behoofe-
ful** useful. **state** ceremony, pomp. 15 **faint** causing faintness.
                                                     101

I 'll call them back again to comfort me.
Nurse!—What should she do here?
My dismal scene I needs must act alone.
Come, vial.   20
What if this mixture do not work at all?
Shall I be marry'd then tomorrow morning?
No, no! this shall forbid it, lie thou there.
What if it be a poison which the Friar
Subtly hath minister'd to have me dead,   25
Lest in this marriage he should be dishonor'd
Because he marry'd me before to Romeo?
I fear it is, and yet methinks it should not,
For he hath still been tried a holy man.
How if, when I am laid into the tomb,   30
I wake before the time that Romeo
Come to redeem me? There 's a fearful point!
Shall I not then be stiffled in the vault,
To whose foul mouth no healthsome air breathes in,
And there die strangled ere my Romeo comes?   35
Or if I live, is it not very like
The horrible conceit of death and night
Together with the terror of the place—
As in a vault, an ancient receptacle,
Where for this many hundred years the bones   40
Of all my bury'd ancestors are pack'd,
Where bloody Tybalt yet but green in earth
Lies fest'ring in his shroud, where as they say
At some hours in the night spirits resort—
Alack, alack, is it not like that I   45

19 **dismal** unlucky. 23 **this, thou** i.e. her dagger. 25 **minister'd**
provided. 29 **still** always. **tried** proved. 33 **stiffled** stifled (pronounced with a short *i*). 37 **conceit** idea. 39 **As** namely. **receptacle**
stressed ´ – ´ –. 40 **this** these (old plural). 42 **green** freshly,
recently.

So early waking—what with loathsome smells
And shrieks like mandrakes torn out of the earth,
That living mortals hearing them run mad—
O if I wake, shall I not be distraught,
Environed with all these hideous fears,   50
And madly play with my forefathers' joints
And pluck the mangled Tybalt from his shroud
And in this rage with some great kinsman's bone
As with a club dash out my desp'rate brains?
O look! methinks I see my cousin's ghost   55
Seeking out Romeo that did spit his body
Upon a rapier's point. Stay Tybalt, stay!
Romeo, Romeo, Romeo! Here's drink—I drink to
     thee.
          ⟨*She falls upon her bed within the curtains.*⟩

[SCENE 4]

Enter Capulet's Wife and Nurse ⟨*with herbs*⟩.

Wife. Hold, take these keys and fetch more spices,
     Nurse.
Nurse. They call for dates and quinces in the
     pastry.

Enter old Capulet.

Capulet. Come, stir, stir, stir! the second cock hath
     crow'd,
The curfew bell hath rung, 'tis three a clock.
Look to the bak'd meats, good Angelica,   5
Spare not for cost.

47 mandrakes N. 49 distraught distracted, driven mad. 53 **rage**
madness. SD **curtains** i.e. of the rear stage. 2 **pastry** pastry room,
pantry. 5 **bak'd meats** meat pies. **Angelica** the Nurse.

Nurse.   Go you cot-quean, go,
Get you to bed. Faith, you 'll be sick tomorrow
For this night's watching.
   Capulet. No, not a whit. What! I have watch'd ere
    now
All night for lesser cause, and ne'er been sick.   10
   Wife. Ay, you have been a mouse-hunt in your time,
But I will watch you from such watching now.
                    Exeunt Wife and Nurse.
   Capulet. A jealous hood, a jealous hood!

     *Enter three or four ⟨Servingmen⟩ with spits
            and logs and baskets.*

Now fellow, what is there?
   1. Servingman. Things for the cook, sir, but I know
    not what.   15
   Capulet. Make haste, make haste.
                   [*Exit 1. Servingman.*]
                Sirrah, fetch drier logs.
Call Peter, he will show thee where they are.
   2. Servingman. I have a head, sir, that will find out
    logs
And never trouble Peter for the matter.   ⟨*Exit.*⟩
   Capulet. Mass! and well said, a merry whoreson,
    ha!   20
Thou shalt be loggerhead. Good faith, 'tis day,
                    Play music.
The County will be here with music straight,
For so he said he would. I hear him near.

6 **cot-quean** man meddling with woman's work (literally 'cottage-wife'). 8 **watching** staying awake. 11 **mouse-hunt** woman-chaser.
12 **watch** prevent. 13 **hood** hud, ninny N. SD ⟨Servingmen⟩ Q1
Servingman; see I.4.1 SD N. 17 **Peter** N. 20 **Mass** by the mass.
whoreson rascal. 21 **loggerhead** blockhead. **faith** Q2 *father.*
   104

Nurse! Wife! What ho! What! Nurse, I say.

Enter Nurse.

Go waken Juliet, go and trim her up,   25
I 'll go and chat with Paris. Hie, make haste,
Make haste, the bridegroom he is come already.
Make haste, I say.   [*Exit.*]
  Nurse. Mistress! what! mistress. Juliet! Fast, I
      warrant her, she.
Why! lamb, why! lady. Fie, you slugabed.   30
Why! love. I say! madam. Sweetheart! Why! bride.
What, not a word? You take your pennyworths now.
Sleep for a week, for the next night I warrant
The County Paris hath set up his rest
That you shall rest but little. God forgive me!   35
Marry and amen! How sound is she asleep.
I needs must wake her. Madam, madam, madam!
Ay, let the County take you in your bed,
He 'll fright you up, i' faith. Will it not be?   39
What! dressed and in your clothes and down again?
I must needs wake you. Lady! lady! lady!
Alas, alas! Help, help! my lady 's dead.
O weraday that ever I was born!
Some *aqua vitae*, ho! My lord, my lady!

          ⟨*Enter Capulet's Wife.*⟩

  Wife. What noise is here?
  Nurse.   O lamentable day!   45
  Wife. What is the matter?
  Nurse.   Look, look! O heavy day!
  Wife. O me, O me! my child, my only life!

29 **Nurse** for staging see N. **Fast** fast asleep. 32 **pennyworths**
i.e. of sleep (pronounced 'penn'orths'). 34 **set up his rest** firmly
resolved N. 43 **weraday** weladay, alas.

Revive, look up, or I will die with thee.
Help, help! Call help!

Enter Capulet.

Capulet. For shame, bring Juliet forth, her lord is
    come.   50
Nurse. She 's dead, deceas'd, she 's dead, alack the
    day!
Wife. Alack the day! she 's dead, she 's dead, she 's
    dead!
Capulet. Ha! let me see her. Out alas! she 's cold.
Her blood is settled and her joints are stiff,
Life and these lips have long been separated.   55
Death lies on her like an untimely frost
Upon the sweetest flow'r of all the field.
Nurse. O lamentable day!
Wife.   O woeful time!
Capulet. Death, that hath tane her hence to make
    me wail,
Ties up my tongue and will not let me speak.   60

Enter Friar and the County.

Friar. Come, is the bride ready to go to church?
Capulet. Ready to go but never to return.
O son, the night before thy wedding day
Hath Death lain with thy wife. There she lies,
Flow'r as she was, deflowered by him.   65
Death is my son-in-law, Death is my heir:
My daughter he hath wedded. I will die
And leave him all: life, living—all is Death's.
Paris. Have I thought long to see this morning's
    face,

54 settled congealed. 68 living property. 69 thought long expected,
hoped. long Q2 *loue.*
    106

And doth it give me such a sight as this?　　　70
　　⟨All at once cry out and wring their hands.⟩
　Wife. Accurs'd, unhappy, wretched, hateful day!
Most miserable hour that e'er Time saw
In lasting labor of his pilgrimage!
But one—poor one, one poor and loving child—
But one thing to rejoice and solace in,　　　75
And cruel Death hath catch'd it from my sight!
　Nurse. O woe! O woeful, woeful, woeful day!
Most lamentable day, most woeful day
That ever ever I did yet behold.
O day, O day, O day! O hateful day!　　　80
Never was seen so black a day as this.
O woeful day! O woeful day!
　Paris. Beguil'd, divorced, wronged, spited, slain!
Most detestable Death, by thee beguil'd,
By cruel cruel thee quite overthrown!　　　85
O love! O life! not life, but love in death!
　Capulet. Despis'd, distressed, hated, martyr'd,
　　kill'd!
Uncomfortable Time, why cam'st thou now
To murther, murther our solemnity?
O child, O child! my soul and not my child!　　　90
Dead art thou. Alack! my child is dead,
And with my child my joys are buried.
　Friar. Peace, ho! for shame! confusion's cure lives
　　not
In these confusions. Heaven and yourself　　　94
Had part in this fair maid; now Heav'n hath all,
And all the better is it for the maid.
Your part in her you could not keep from death,

---

76 **catch'd** snatched. 84 **detestable** stressed ⌣ – ⌣́ –. 88 **Uncomfortable** discomforting. 93 **confusion** disaster. **cure** Q2 *care.*

But Heav'n keeps his part in eternal life.
The most you sought was her promotion,
For 'twas your Heaven she should be advanc'd.   100
And weep ye now, seeing she is advanc'd
Above the clouds as high as Heav'n itself?
O in this love you love your child so ill
That you run mad, seeing that she is well.
She 's not well marry'd that lives marry'd long,   105
But she 's best marry'd that dies marry'd young.
Dry up your tears and stick your rosemary
On this fair corse, and as the custom is,
And in her best array, bear her to church;
For though fond Nature bids us all lament,   110
Yet Nature's tears are Reason's merriment.
   Capulet. All things that we ordained festival
Turn from their office to black funeral—
Our instruments to melancholy bells,
Our wedding cheer to a sad burial feast,   115
Our solemn hymns to sullen dirges change,
Our bridal flow'rs serve for a bury'd corse,
And all things change them to the contrary.
   Friar. Sir go you in, and madam go with him,
And go, Sir Paris. Everyone prepare   120
To follow this fair corse unto her grave.
The Heav'ns do low'r upon you for some ill,
Move them no more by crossing their high will.
       ⟨*They all but the Nurse go forth, casting
       rosemary on her and shutting the curtains.*

                Enter Musicians.⟩

100 **advanc'd** i.e. in rank by marriage. 101 **advanc'd** raised. 104
well i.e. in Heaven. 107 **rosemary** N. 110 **fond** Q2 *some*. **Nature**
natural feeling. 113 **office** function. 115 **cheer** food. SD ⟨**They all
. . . Musicians**⟩ Q2 *Exeunt manet* N.
    108

1. Musician. Faith, we may put up our pipes and
be gone.   125

Nurse. Honest good fellows, ah put up, put up!
For well you know this is a pitiful case.

1. Musician. Ay, by my troth, the case may be
amended.   *Exit Nurse.*

Enter Peter.

Peter. Musicians, O Musicians—'Heart's Ease,'
'Heart's Ease.' O and you will have me live, play
'Heart's Ease.'   132

1. Musician. Why 'Heart's Ease'?

Peter. O Musicians, because my heart itself plays
'My Heart is Full'—O play me some merry dump to
comfort me.   136

Musicians. Not a dump, we, 'tis no time to play
now.

Peter. You will not then?

1. Musician. No.   140

Peter. I will then give it you soundly.

1. Musician. What will you give us?

Peter. No money, on my faith, but the gleek. I will
give you the 'Minstrel.'   144

1. Musician. Then will I give you the 'Serving
Creature.'

Peter. Then will I lay the serving-creature's dagger

124 **put up our pipes** put away our instruments (proverbial for
'cease'). 127 **case** event. 128 **case** quibble on 'instrument case.'
129 **amended** bettered. SD Nurse Q2 *omnes.* SD Peter Q2 *Will
Kemp* N. 130 **'Heart's Ease'** a popular tune called for in the
old play *Misogonus*. 135 **'My Heart is Full'** N. **dump** mournful
tune. 141 **give it you** let you have it. **soundly** forcefully (quibble
on 'with sounds'). 143 **gleek** jeer. 144 **give you** call you (as in a
formal insult; compare II.3.27 N).

on your pate. I will carry no crotchets. I 'll *re* you,
I 'll *fa* you, do you note me?   149

1. Musician. And you *re* us and *fa* us you note us.

2. Musician. Pray you put up your dagger and
put out your wit. Then have at you with my wit.

Peter. I will dry-beat you with an iron wit and put
up my iron dagger. Answer me like men:

> When griping griefs the heart doth wound,   155
> (And doleful dumps the mind oppress,)
> Then music with her silver sound—

Why 'silver sound'? Why 'music with her silver
sound'? What say you, Simon Catling?

1. Musician. Marry, sir, because silver hath a sweet
sound.   161

Peter. Prates. What say you, Hugh Rebeck?

2. Musician. I say 'silver sound' because musicians
sound for silver.

Peter. Prates too. What say you, James Sound-
post?   166

3. Musician. Faith, I know not what to say.

Peter. O I cry you mercy, you are the singer. I will
'say' for you. It is 'music with her silver sound' because musicians have no gold for sounding.   170

> —Then music with her silver sound
> With speedy help doth lend redress.

Exit.

148 **carry** endure. **crotchets** whims (quibble on 'quarter notes').
148–9 **re . . . fa you** N. 149 **note** pay attention to. 150 **note us**
set us to music. 152 **put out** display. 155–7 **When . . . sound** N.
156 **dumps** sorrows. 159 **Catling** lute string of catgut. 162 **Prates**
the subject 'he' is understood. **Rebeck** three-stringed fiddle. 165
Sound-post peg supporting the body of a stringed instrument.
168 **cry you mercy** beg your pardon. 170 **sounding** playing.

1. Musician. What a pestilent knave is this same!
2. Musician. Hang him, Jack. Come, we 'll in here,
tarry for the mourners, and stay dinner.   *Exeunt.*

175 **stay** wait for.

[*Act V*

SCENE 1]

Enter Romeo.

Romeo. If I may trust the flatt'ring truth of sleep
My dreams presage some joyful news at hand.
My bosom's lord sits lightly in his throne,
And all this day an unaccustom'd spirit
Lifts me above the ground with cheerful thoughts. 5
I dreamt my lady came and found me dead
(Strange dream that gives a dead man leave to
    think!)
And breath'd such life with kisses in my lips
That I reviv'd and was an emperor.
Ah me! how sweet is love itself possess'd   10
When but love's shadows are so rich in joy.

Enter Romeo's Man ⟨*Balthasar, booted*⟩.

News from Verona! How now, Balthasar?
Dost thou not bring me letters from the Friar?
How doth my lady? Is my father well?
How fares my Juliet? That I ask again,   15
For nothing can be ill if she be well.
  Balthasar. Then she is well and nothing can be ill.
Her body sleeps in Capels' monument,
And her immortal part with angels lives.

1 **flatt'ring** illusive. 3 **bosom's lord** i.e. heart. 11 **shadows** images.
SD **booted** i.e. for riding. 15 **fares my Juliet** Q1; Q2 *doth my Lady
Iuliet* N. 18 **monument** burial vault.

I saw her laid low in her kindred's vault   20
And presently took post to tell it you.
O pardon me for bringing these ill news,
Since you did leave it for my office, sir.
 Romeo. Is it in so? Then I defy you, stars!
Thou know'st my lodging. Get me ink and paper   25
And hire post horses. I will hence tonight.
 Balthasar. I do beseech you, sir, have patience,
Your looks are pale and wild and do import
Some misadventure.
 Romeo.   Tush, thou art deceiv'd.
Leave me and do the thing I bid thee do.   30
Hast thou no letters to me from the Friar?
 Balthasar. No my good lord.
 Romeo.   No matter, get thee gone
And hire those horses. I 'll be with thee straight.
        Exit ⟨Balthasar⟩.
Well Juliet, I will lie with thee tonight.
Let 's see for means. O mischief, thou art swift   35
To enter in the thoughts of desp'rate men.
I do remember an apothecary,
And hereabouts 'a dwells (which late I noted)
In tatter'd weeds with overwhelming brows,
Culling of simples. Meager were his looks,   40
Sharp misery had worn him to the bones.
And in his needy shop a tortoise hung,
An alligator stuff'd and other skins
Of ill-shap'd fishes; and about his shelves
A beggarly account of empty boxes,   45

21 **took post** traveled by post horse. 24 **in** e'en N. **defy** Q1; Q2
denie. 27 **patience** here pronounced 'pati-ence'; see I.4.94 N. 39
weeds clothes. **overwhelming** beetling. 40 **simples** medicinal
herbs. 45 **account** reckoning, number.

Green earthen pots, bladders and musty seeds,
Remnants of packthread and old cakes of roses
Were thinly scatter'd to make up a show.
Noting this penury, to myself I said,
'And if a man did need a poison now   50
Whose sale is present death in Mantua,
Here lives a caitiff wretch would sell it him.'
O this same thought did but forerun my need,
And this same needy man must sell it me.
As I remember, this should be the house,   55
Being holy day, the beggar's shop is shut.
What ho! apothecary!

⟨*Enter Apothecary.*⟩

Apothecary.   Who calls so loud?
Romeo. Come hither man, I see that thou art poor.
Hold, there is forty ducats. Let me have
A dram of poison, such soon-speeding gear   60
As will disperse itself through all the veins
That the life-weary taker may fall dead,
And that the trunk may be discharg'd of breath
As violently as hasty powder fired
Doth hurry from the fatal cannon's womb.   65
Apothecary. Such mortal drugs I have, but Man-
          tua's law
Is death to any he that utters them.
Romeo. Art thou so bare and full of wretchedness,
And fear'st to die? Famine is in thy cheeks,
Need and oppression starveth in thy eyes,   70
Contempt and begg'ry hangs upon thy back.

---

47 **cakes of roses** caked rose petals (for use as perfume). 52 **caitiff**
miserable. 59 **ducats** gold coins. 60 **gear** stuff. 63 **trunk** body.
67 **utters** gives out. 70 **starveth in** look out hungrily from.

114

The world is not thy friend nor the world's law,
The world affords no law to make thee rich—
Then be not poor, but break it and take this.   74
  Apothecary. My poverty but not my will consents.
  Romeo. I pay thy poverty and not thy will.
  Apothecary. Put this in any liquid thing you will
And drink it off, and if you had the strength
Of twenty men it would dispatch you straight.
  Romeo. There is thy gold—worse poison to men's
    souls,   80
Doing more murther in this loathsome world
Than these poor compounds that thou mayst not
    sell.
I sell thee poison, thou hast sold me none.
Farewell, buy food and get thyself in flesh.
Come cordial, and not poison, go with me   85
To Juliet's grave, for there must I use thee.   *Exeunt.*

[SCENE 2]

Enter Friar John.

  John. Holy Franciscan Friar! brother, ho!

Enter Lawrence.

  Lawrence. This same should be the voice of Friar
    John.
Welcome from Mantua, what says Romeo?
Or if his mind be writ give me his letter.
  John. Going to find a barefoot brother out,   5
One of our order to associate me,

76 pay Q1; Q2 *pray.* 85 **cordial** restorative. SD **Enter Friar John**
so Q1; Q2 *Enter Frier Iohn to Frier Lawrence* N. 6 **associate**
accompany N.

Here in this city visiting the sick,
And finding him, the searchers of the town,
Suspecting that we both were in a house
Where the infectious pestilence did reign,   10
Seal'd up the doors and would not let us forth,
So that my speed to Mantua there was stay'd.
   Lawrence. Who bare my letter then to Romeo?
   John. I could not send it (here it is again)
Nor get a messenger to bring it thee,   15
So fearful were they of infection.
   Lawrence. Unhappy fortune! By my brotherhood,
The letter was not nice but full of charge,
Of dear import, and the neglecting it
May do much danger. Friar John, go hence,   20
Get me an iron crow and bring it straight
Unto my cell.
   John. Brother, I 'll go and bring it thee.   *Exit.*
   Lawrence. Now must I to the monument alone,
Within this three hours will fair Juliet wake.   25
She will beshrew me much that Romeo
Hath had no notice of these accidents—
But I will write again to Mantua
And keep her at my cell till Romeo come.
Poor living corse, clos'd in a dead man's tomb.   *Exit.*

8 **searchers** health officers. 11 **Seal'd up the doors** N. 12 **stay'd** stopped. 18 **nice** trivial. **charge** weight, importance. 21 **crow** crowbar. 26 **beshrew** censure.

116

[SCENE 3]

Enter Paris and his Page ⟨with flowers and sweet water⟩.

Paris. Give me thy torch, boy, hence and stand
    aloof.
Yet put it out, for I would not be seen.
Under yond yew trees lay thee all along,
Holding thy ear close to the hollow ground,
So shall no foot upon the churchyard tread   5
(Being loose, unfirm with digging up of graves)
But thou shalt hear it. Whistle then to me
As signal that thou hear'st something approach.
Give me those flowers, do as I bid thee, go.
    Page. I am almost afraid to stand alone   10
Here in the churchyard, yet I will adventure.

                      [Retires.]
          ⟨*Paris strews the tomb with flowers.*⟩
    Paris. Sweet flow'r, with flow'rs thy bridal bed I
    strew.
O woe, thy canopy is dust and stones
Which with sweet water nightly I will dew,
Or wanting that, with tears distill'd by moans.   15
The obsequies that I for thee will keep
Nightly shall be to strew thy grave and weep.

                      Whistle Page.
The boy gives warning something doth approach.
What cursed foot wanders this way tonight
To cross my obsequies and true love's rite?   20

3 yew Q1; Q2 *young*. yew trees symbolic of mourning. **all along**
at full length. 11 **adventure** take the risk. 13 **canopy** covering.
14 **sweet** perfumed. 20 **cross** thwart.

What! with a torch? Muffle me, night, awhile.

[*Retires.*]

Enter Romeo and Balthasar ⟨*with a torch,
a mattock and a crow of iron*⟩.

Romeo. Give me that mattock and the wrenching
iron.
Hold, take this letter, early in the morning
See thou deliver it to my lord and father.
Give me the light. Upon thy life I charge thee,   25
Whate'er thou hear'st or see'st, stand all aloof
And do not interrupt me in my course.
Why I descend into this bed of Death
Is partly to behold my lady's face,   29
But chiefly to take thence from her dead finger
A precious ring—a ring that I must use
In dear employment. Therefore hence, be gone.
But if thou jealous dost return to pry
In what I farther shall intend to do,
By Heaven I will tear thee joint by joint   35
And strew this hungry churchyard with thy limbs.
The time and my intents are savage-wild,
More fierce and more inexorable far
Than empty tigers or the roaring sea.
Balthasar. I will be gone sir, and not trouble ye.
Romeo. So shalt thou show me friendship. Take
thou that,   41
Live and be prosperous. And farewell, good fellow.
Balthasar. For all this same I'll hide me hereabout,
His looks I fear and his intents I doubt.   [*Retires.*]
Romeo. Thou detestable maw, thou womb of death,

21 **Muffle** hide. SD **Balthasar** Q1; Q2 *Peter* N. 32 **dear** important.
33 **jealous** suspicious. 44 **doubt** suspect. 45 **detestable** stressed
⏑ – ⏑ –. **maw** stomach. **womb** belly.
118

Gorg'd with the dearest morsel of the earth,   46
Thus I enforce thy rotten jaws to open,
And in despite I 'll cram thee with more food.
                      ⟨*Romeo opens the tomb.*⟩
  Paris. This is that banish'd haughty Montague
That murder'd my love's cousin (with which grief
It is supposed the fair creature died)   51
And here is come to do some villainous shame
To the dead bodies. I will apprehend him.
Stop thy unhallow'd toil, vile Montague!
Can vengeance be pursu'd further than death?   55
Condemned villain, I do apprehend thee.
Obey and go with me, for thou must die.
  Romeo. I must indeed and therefore came I hither.
Good gentle youth, tempt not a desp'rate man,
Fly hence and leave me. Think upon these gone,   60
Let them affright thee. I beseech thee, youth,
Put not another sin upon my head
By urging me to fury. O be gone!
By Heav'n, I love thee better than myself,
For I come hither arm'd against myself.   65
Stay not, be gone! live, and hereafter say
A mad man's mercy bid thee run away.
  Paris. I do defy thy conjuration
And apprehend thee for a felon here.   69
  Romeo. Wilt thou provoke me? then have at thee,
    boy!   ⟨*They fight.*⟩
  Page. O Lord, they fight! I will go call the watch.
                                [*Exit.*]
  Paris. O I am slain! If thou be merciful
Open the tomb, lay me with Juliet.

48 **despite** defiance. SD **tomb** represented by the rear stage.
68 **conjuration** Q2 *commiration;* Q1 *coniurations;* entreaty. 71
Page Q2 omits; Q1 *Boy.*

Romeo. In faith, I will. Let me peruse this face.
Mercutio's kinsman, noble County Paris!   75
What said my man when my betossed soul
Did not attend him as we rode? I think
He told me Paris should have marry'd Juliet.
Said he not so? or did I dream it so?
Or am I mad, hearing him talk of Juliet,   80
To think it was so? O give me thy hand,
One writ with me in sour Misfortune's book.
I 'll bury thee in a triumphant grave.
A grave? O no, a lanthorn, slaughter'd youth,
For here lies Juliet, and her beauty makes   85
This vault a feasting presence full of light.
Death, lie thou there, by a dead man interr'd.
How oft when men are at the point of death
Have they been merry—which their keepers call
A lightning before death. O how may I   90
Call this a lightning? O my love, my wife!
Death that hath suck'd the honey of thy breath
Hath had no power yet upon thy beauty.
Thou art not conquer'd—Beauty's ensign yet
Is crimson in thy lips and in thy cheeks,   95
And Death's pale flag is not advanced there.
Tybalt, ly'st thou there in thy bloody sheet?
O what more favor can I do to thee
Than with that hand that cut thy youth in twain
To sunder his that was thine enemy?   100
Forgive me, cousin. Ah dear Juliet,
Why art thou yet so fair? shall I believe

83 **triumphant** magnificent. 84 **lanthorn** lantern (windowed dome).
86 **feasting** festive. **presence** presence chamber. 87 **Death** i.e.
Paris' body. 89 **keepers** nurses. 90 **lightning** lightening of spirits
(quibble on 'shedding of light'). 102 **shall I believe** Q2 *I will
beleeue, Shall I beleeue* N.

120

That unsubstantial Death is amorous
And that the lean abhorred monster keeps
Thee here in dark to be his paramour? 105
For fear of that I still will stay with thee
And never from this pallet of dim Night
Depart again, here, here will I remain
With worms that are thy chambermaids, O here
Will I set up my everlasting rest 110
And shake the yoke of inauspicious stars
From this world-weary'd flesh. Eyes look your last,
Arms take your last embrace, and lips (O you
The doors of breath) seal with a righteous kiss
A dateless bargain to engrossing Death! 115
Come bitter conduct, come unsav'ry guide,
Thou desp'rate pilot, now at once run on
The dashing rocks thy seasick weary bark.
Here 's to my love! O true apothecary, 119
Thy drugs are quick. Thus with a kiss I die. ⟨*Falls.*⟩

Enter Friar with lanthorn, crow and spade.

Friar. Saint Francis be my speed! how oft tonight
Have my old feet stumbled at graves. Who 's there?
Balthasar. Here 's one, a friend, and one that knows
    you well.
Friar. Bliss be upon you. Tell me, good my friend,
What torch is yond that vainly lends his light 125
To grubs and eyeless skulls? as I discern,
It burneth in the Capels' monument.

107 **pallet** N. 108–20 **Depart again . . . I die** for text see II.1.
230–3 N. 110 **rest** repose (for quibble see IV.4.34 N). 115 **dateless** endless. **engrossing** buying up in gross, monopolizing. 116
conduct guide. 121 **speed** aid, protector. 122 **stumbled** an ill omen.
125 **vainly** uselessly.

Balthasar. It doth so, holy sir, and there 's my
    master,
One that you love.
    Friar.   Who is it?
    Balthasar.   Romeo.   129
    Friar. How long hath he been there?
    Balthasar.   Full half an hour.
    Friar. Go with me to the vault.
    Balthasar.   I dare not, sir,
My master knows not but I am gone hence,
And fearfully did menace me with death
If I did stay to look on his intents.   134
    Friar. Stay then, I 'll go alone. Fear comes upon me,
O much I fear some ill unthrifty thing.
    Balthasar. As I did sleep under this yew tree here
I dreamt my master and another fought
And that my master slew him.   *[Exit]*.
    Friar.   Romeo!
⟨*Friar stoops and looks on the blood and weapons.*⟩
Alack alack, what blood is this which stains   140
The stony entrance of this sepulcher?
What mean these masterless and gory swords
To lie discolor'd by this place of peace?
Romeo, O pale! Who else? what! Paris too?
And steep'd in blood? Ah what an unkind hour   145
Is guilty of this lamentable chance.
The lady stirs.   ⟨*Juliet rises.*⟩
    Juliet. O comfortable Friar, where is my lord?
I do remember well where I should be
And there I am, where is my Romeo?   150
    Friar. I hear some noise, lady, come from that nest
Of death, contagion and unnatural sleep.

136 **unthrifty** unlucky. 137 **yew** Q2 *yong.* 145 **unkind** unnatural,
degenerate (stressed ´ –). 148 **comfortable** comforting.
    122

A greater power than we can contradict
Hath thwarted our intents, come, come away.
Thy husband in thy bosom there lies dead,   155
And Paris too. Come, I'll dispose of thee
Among a sisterhood of holy nuns.
Stay not to question, for the watch is coming.
Come go, good Juliet, I dare no longer stay.   *Exit.*
  Juliet. Go get thee hence, for I will not away.   160
What 's here? a cup clos'd in my true love's hand!
Poison I see hath been his timeless end.
O churl, drunk all and left no friendly drop
To help me after? I will kiss thy lips,
Haply some poison yet doth hang on them   165
To make me die with a restorative.
Thy lips are warm.

Enter Page and Watch.

  Chief Watchman. Lead boy, which way?
  Juliet. Yea noise? then I 'll be brief. O happy
    dagger,
This is thy sheath—there rust and let me die.   170
                    ⟨*She stabs herself and falls.*⟩
  Page. This is the place, there where the torch doth
    burn.
  Chief Watchman. The ground is bloody, search
    about the churchyard.
Go, some of you, whoe'er you find attach.
                    [*Exeunt some of the Watch.*]
Pitiful sight! here lies the County slain,
And Juliet bleeding, warm and newly dead,   175
Who here hath lain this two days buried.

162 **timeless** untimely. 163 **churl** miser. 171 **Page** Q2 *Watch boy.*
173 **attach** arrest. 176 **this** these.

Go tell the Prince, run to the Capulets,
Raise up the Montagues, some others search.

> *[Exeunt others of the Watch.]*

We see the ground whereon these woes do lie,
But the true ground of all these piteous woes   180
We cannot without circumstance descry.

Enter Romeo's Man [and a Watchman].

2. Watchman. Here 's Romeo's man, we found him
   in the churchyard.
Chief Watchman. Hold him in safety till the Prince
   come hither.

Enter Friar and another Watchman.

3. Watchman. Here is a friar that trembles, sighs
   and weeps,
We took this mattock and this spade from him   185
As he was coming from this churchyard's side.
Chief Watchman. A great suspicion, stay the friar
   too.

Enter the Prince ⟨with [Citizens and] others⟩.

Prince. What misadventure is so early up
That calls our person from our morning rest?

Enter Capels.

Capulet. What should it be that is so shriek'd
   abroad?   190
Wife. The people in the street cry 'Romeo,'
Some 'Juliet' and some 'Paris,' and all run

---

179 **woes** i.e. piteous bodies. 180 **ground** basis, cause. 181 **circumstance** details. 187 **stay** detain. SD **Citizens** N. SD **Enter Capels** N. 190 **shriek'd** Q2 *shrike.* 191 **The people** Q2 *O the people;* for text see V.3.102 N.

With open outcry toward our monument.

  Prince. What fear is this which startles in our ears?

  Chief Watchman. Sovereign, here lies the County
    Paris slain,   195

And Romeo dead, and Juliet, dead before,

Warm and new kill'd.

  Prince. Search, seek, and know how this foul mur-
    der comes.

  Chief Watchman. Here is a friar and slaughter'd
    Romeo's man,

With instruments upon them fit to open   200

These dead men's tombs.

  Capulet. O Heav'ns! O Wife, look how our daughter
    bleeds!

This dagger hath mistane, for lo his house

Is empty on the back of Montague,

And it mis-sheathed in my daughter's bosom.   205

  Wife. O me! this sight of death is as a bell

That warns my old age to a sepulcher.

Enter Montague.

  Prince. Come Montague, for thou art early up

To see thy son and heir now early down.   209

  Montague. Alas my liege, my wife is dead tonight,

Grief of my son's exile hath stopp'd her breath.

What further woe conspires against mine age?

  Prince. Look and thou shalt see.

  Montague. O thou untaught! what manners is in
    this,

To press before thy father to a grave?   215

  Prince. Seal up the mouth of outrage for a while

194 **our** Q2 *your;* i.e. the Prince's (royal plural). 199 **slaughter'd**
Q2 *Slaughter.* 203 **mistane** mistaken, gone astray. 207 **warns**
summons. 216 **Seal up** for staging see N. **mouth of outrage** im-
moderate clamoring.

Till we can clear these ambiguities
And know their spring, their head, their true descent,
And then will I be gen'ral of your woes
And lead you e'en to death. Meantime forbear,   220
And let mischance be slave to patience.
Bring forth the parties of suspicion.
  Friar. I am, the greatest, able to do least,
Yet most suspected, as the time and place
Doth make against me, of this direful murther;   225
And here I stand both to impeach and purge
Myself condemned and myself excus'd.
  Prince. Then say at once what thou dost know in
    this.
  Friar. I will be brief, for my short date of breath
Is not so long as is a tedious tale.   230
Romeo there dead was husband to that Juliet,
And she there dead, that Romeo's faithful wife,
I marry'd them; and their stol'n marriage day
Was Tybalt's doomsday, whose untimely death   234
Banish'd the new-made bridegroom from this city,
For whom and not for Tybalt Juliet pin'd.
You to remove that siege of grief from her
Betroth'd and would have marry'd her perforce
To County Paris. Then comes she to me
And with wild looks bid me devise some mean   240
To rid her from this second marriage,
Or in my cell there would she kill herself.
Then gave I her, so tutor'd by my art,
A sleeping potion which so took effect
As I intended, for it wrought on her   245
The form of death. Meantime I writ to Romeo

222 of under. 224 as considering how. 225 **make against** implicate.
226 **purge** exonerate. 229 **date of breath** time of life. 232 **that** Q1;
Q2 *thats.*
   126

That he should hither come as this dire night
To help to take her from her borrow'd grave,
Being the time the potion's force should cease.
But he which bore my letter, Friar John,   250
Was stay'd by accident and yesternight
Return'd my letter back. Then all alone
At the prefixed hour of her waking
Came I to take her from her kindred's vault,
Meaning to keep her closely at my cell   255
Till I conveniently could send to Romeo.
But when I came some minute ere the time
Of her awak'ning, here untimely lay
The noble Paris and true Romeo dead.
She wakes, and I entreated her come forth   260
And bear this work of Heav'n with patience,
But then a noise did scare me from the tomb
And she too desp'rate would not go with me,
But as it seems did violence on herself.
All this I know, and to the marriage   265
Her nurse is privy; and if aught in this
Miscarry'd by my fault, let my old life
Be sacrific'd some hour before his time
Unto the rigor of severest law.   269
  Prince. We still have known thee for a holy man.
Where 's Romeo's man? what can he say to this?
  Balthasar. I brought my master news of Juliet's
    death,
And then in post he came from Mantua
To this same place, to this same monument.
This letter he early bid me give his father   275
And threaten'd me with death, going in the vault,
If I departed not and left him there.

247 **as this** this. 255 **closely** secretly. 266 **privy** secretly accessory.
273 **in post** posthaste.

Prince. Give me the letter, I will look on it.
Where is the County's page that rais'd the watch?
Sirrah, what made your master in this place?   280
Page. He came with flow'rs to strew his lady's grave
And bid me stand aloof, and so I did.
Anon comes one with light to ope the tomb,
And by and by my master drew on him,
And then I ran away to call the watch.   285
Prince. This letter doth make good the Friar's
        words—
Their course of love, the tidings of her death;
And here he writes that he did buy a poison
Of a poor pothecary, and therewithal
Came to this vault to die and lie with Juliet.   290
Where be these enemies? Capulet! Montague!
See what a scourge is laid upon your hate
That Heav'n finds means to kill your joys with love.
And I for winking at your discords too
Have lost a brace of kinsmen. All are punish'd.   295
Capulet. O brother Montague, give me thy hand.
This is my daughter's jointure, for no more
Can I demand.
Montague.   But I can give thee more,
For I will ray her statue in pure gold
That whiles Verona by that name is known   300
There shall no figure at such rate be set
As that of true and faithful Juliet.
Capulet. As rich shall Romeo's by his lady's lie,
Poor sacrifices of our enmity.

280 **made** was doing. 289 **therewithal** therewith, along with that.
294–5 **And I for winking . . . punish'd** see I.1.99–100 N. 295
a brace of kinsmen i.e. Mercutio and Paris. 297 **jointure** marriage
settlement N. 299 **ray** array, bedeck (i.e. gild) N. 301 **rate** value.

Prince. A glooming peace this morning with it brings,   305
The Sun for sorrow will not show his head.
Go hence to have more talk of these sad things:
Some shall be pardon'd and some punished.
For never was a story of more woe
Than this of Juliet and her Romeo.   [*Exeunt.*]

FINIS.

NOTES

The Prologue

The Prologue Here and in several other plays Shakespeare employs the classical device of commenting on his theme through a Prologue spoken by an actor called the Chorus. He satirizes the convention at I.4.7–8.

12 two hours It was possible to perform an Elizabethan play in approximately such a short space of time chiefly because of the absence, in an Elizabethan public playhouse, of pauses for dropping a curtain or shifting scenery. Shakespeare mentions the same length of time in the Prologue to *Henry VIII*, where the Chorus advises certain members of the audience that they 'may see away their shilling Richly in two short hours.' (Shakespeare quotations are from G. L. Kittredge's edition of 1936.)

Act I, Scene 1

Act I, Scene 1 In Elizabethan editions of *Romeo and Juliet* there are no act and scene divisions, which originate with Shakespeare's 18th-century editors. The present edition retains the traditional divisions, except at three points where the action is continuous. See notes at I.4.114, II.1.43, and IV.4.29.

1–11 coals . . . move Sampson's and Gregory's quibbles and puns on *coals*, *colliers*, *choler*, *draw* ('draw swords,' 'pull,' and 'extract'), *collar* ('harness' and 'hangman's noose'), and *moved* ('angered,' 'impelled,' and 'removed') represent a kind of wit popular in the 1590's. Compare I.4.12–21 N.

15 take the wall Since there were no sidewalks and Renaissance streets were usually narrow and littered with filth, in passing someone it was courteous to 'give the wall' to him but insulting to 'take the wall' of him, thus causing him to step into the gutter in the middle of the street.

46 bite my thumb A defiantly insulting gesture made by snicking the thumbnail from under the upper teeth.

60 SD Benvolio This name, meaning literally in Italian 'I wish well,' is one of Shakespeare's additions to his source material.

130

63–83 **Yes, better, sir . . . seek a foe** The action of these lines, omitted from Q1, is represented in that edition by the following stage direction: 'They draw. To them enters Tybalt. They fight. To them the Prince, old Montague and his Wife, old Capulet and his Wife, and other Citizens, and part them.'

76 **Citizens** Editors usually include an Officer with the Citizens entering after l. 75, on the evidence of Q2's speech heading *Offi.* However, this would appear to be the Q2 compositor's misreading of *Citti.*, the parts of ll. 76–7 being 'confused cries' to be assigned to various supernumeraries in the crowd of Citizens. Compare the Q2 speech heading *Citti.* at III.1.141.

78 **long sword** Capulet calls for the old fashioned medieval weapon rather than the newfangled rapier introduced from the continent to England in Elizabethan times. See II.3.28 N.

79 SD **Enter old Montague . . . Wife** Editors usually follow Q2 in locating this direction after l. 81, but the dialogue indicates that Montague is already on stage by l. 80.

99–100 **If ever you disturb . . . the peace** According to Renaissance political theory, the Prince's clemency at this point is an error of civil policy, as he himself later recognizes. (Compare III.1.201 N and V.3.294–5.) Machiavelli, for example, in discussing the problem of restoring unity to a divided city, lists three courses of action open to the civil governor: 'the one is to put the leaders [of the opposing factions] to death . . . or to banish them from the city, or to reconcile them to each other under a pledge not to offend again. Of these three ways, the last is the worst, being the least certain and effective; for it is impossible that, after dissensions that have caused so much bloodshed and other outrages, a forced peace should be enduring. The parties meeting each other daily face to face will with difficulty abstain from mutual insults, and in their daily intercourse fresh causes for quarrel will constantly occur.' (*Discourses on the First Ten Books of Titus Livius*, 3, 27, in *The Prince and the Discourses*, Modern Library ed., New York, 1940, p. 490.)

134–45 **Many a morning . . . remove** Montague's description of his son's romantic melancholy parodies the posturing required of the courtly lover. Compare Rosalind's description of 'a man in love' (*As You Like It*, III.2.392–403) and Ophelia's account of

131

Hamlet's 'madness,' which Polonius pronounces to be 'the very ecstasy of love' (*Hamlet*, II.1.77–100).

152 **so secret and so close** Like a true courtly lover, Romeo cherishes the precept laid down by Andreas Capellanus in *The Art of Courtly Love* (c. 1184), 'Qui non celat, amare non potest' (He who does not conceal his love cannot love). See E. C. Pettet, *Shakespeare and the Romance Tradition*, London, 1949, p. 114.

179–84 **brawling love . . . sleep** The oxymorons and balanced antitheses of these lines are characteristic of Elizabethan sonnets written in the tradition of Petrarchan love poetry. Juliet employs similar conceits at III.2.73–9.

200 **left** Editors usually follow Q2 in here reading *lost*, but in his edition of 1875 P. A. Daniel emends the Q2 reading to *left*, citing two other instances in Shakespeare of a compositor's confusing *left* and *lost* through the similarity in Elizabethan script of *e* to *o* and of *f* to long *s*. The emendation to *left* reveals Romeo's play on Benvolio's *leave* in l. 199, and emphasizes the neo-Platonic idea that Romeo's soul has left his body.

218–19 **rich . . . store** That is, rich as she is in beauty, she is poor in that (being chaste) she will leave no children after death to inherit and perpetuate her wealth of beauty. Compare Sonnets 1–14.

Act I, Scene 2

13 **marr'd . . . made** Capulet uses the common Elizabethan antithesis of 'make' and 'mar' (compare II.3.121), and through a pun on 'married' plays on the proverbial expression, 'Soon married, soon marred.' Compare Parolles: 'A young man married is a man that's marr'd' (*All's Well That Ends Well*, II.3.315).

39–41 **shoemaker . . . nets** The Servant's confusion in the matter of tools and his bawdy quibble on *meddle* are the stock in trade of Elizabethan clowns.

52 **plantain leaf** This was popularly believed to cure poisonous infections but was also applied to cuts and bruises. Romeo implies that Benvolio's proposed cure of love by counterinfection will be no more efficacious than a barked shin, since the same medication cures both ailments.

55–7 **bound . . . tormented** Romeo describes the customary

Elizabethan treatment of lunatics. Compare Malvolio's treatment in *Twelfth Night* (III.4 and IV.2).

71 and Since the Q2 text from about I.2.54 to I.3.36 was printed from an uncorrected exemplar of Q1, Q2's omission of *and* at I.2.71 and the Q2 reading *you* at l. 80 would appear to be the compositor's errors of transmission. Accordingly, at I.2.71 and 80 the present editor prints the Q1 variants *and* and *thee*, the only substantive readings. Two other Q2 variants within this passage (*an* at I.3.13—Q1 *a*—and *the* at l. 33—omitted from Q1) are accepted as necessary corrections of the substantive Q1 text. See G. I. Duthie, 'The Text of Shakespeare's *Romeo and Juliet*,' *Studies in Bibliography*, *4* (1952), pp. 22–3.

76 to supper Editors usually shift this phrase to the Servant's speech immediately following. However, the present editor follows Edward Dowden, who retains the Q2 arrangement in his edition of 1900, interpreting Romeo's 'Whither? to supper?' as an interruption of the Servant's 'Up—to our house.' Since Q1 is the only substantive source of this section of the text, the passag emay well be corrupt beyond editorial redemption.

83 crush The expression 'to crush' a cup of wine or a pot of ale was proverbial. Compare Shallow: 'By the mass, you'll crack a quart together' (*2 Henry IV*, V.3.66–7).

91–4 devout religion . . . heretics Conceits based on the idea of love as religion are typical of Petrarchan love poetry. Romeo uses the same convention when he first meets Juliet (see I.4.212–17 N).

Act I, Scene 3

3–5 Now . . . Juliet Since the 18th century, editors have generally printed this and the Nurse's other speeches in I.3 as verse. However, both aesthetic considerations and bibliographical evidence suggest that their prose arrangement in Q2 and Q1 is more probably correct than incorrect. See Richard Hosley, 'The Corrupting Influence of the Bad Quarto on the Received Text of *Romeo and Juliet*,' *Shakespeare Quarterly*, *4* (1953), 24–5. This article will be hereafter referred to as 'The Received Text.'

5 SD Juliet Since Juliet was born on Lammas Eve or July 31 (see l. 20), her name is appropriate to her birth month.

12 **a pretty age** To Elizabethans a girl's fourteenth birthday made her ripe for marriage. See T. W. Baldwin, *Shakspere's Five-Act Structure*, The University of Illinois Press, 1947, pp. 773–5.

17 **Lammas-tide** The *Lammas* (literally 'loaf-mass') was an old English harvest festival at which loaves of bread made from the new wheat were consecrated.

25 **since . . . eleven years** If this is a topical allusion to the earthquake felt in London on April 6, 1580, it may date *Romeo and Juliet* as early as 1591.

33 **'Shake!'** The action of the dovehouse at the moment of the earthquake, as though spoken by the personified dovehouse.

42 **by my holidam** This expression was originally an oath by a sacred relic, *holidam* being a form of *halidom*, 'sanctity, holy relic.' The form *holidam* was often misunderstood as 'Holy Dame,' the Virgin Mary.

71–2 **I was your mother . . . maid** Since the sight of her daughter's bleeding body will be as a bell that warns her old age to a sepulcher (V.3.206–7), this remark by Capulet's Wife that she is around twenty-eight years old is evidently a falsehood.

79 **This night . . . feast** Editors usually stop this line with a period, but in Q2 it is lightly connected by a comma with the following six lines, the verbs of which are apparently futures prophesying how Juliet will fall in love rather than imperatives commanding her to fall in love.

99 **the guests are come** On the domestic arrangements of the Capulet household see Tucker Brooke, 'Shakespeare Remembers his Youth in Stratford,' in *Essays on Shakespeare and Other Elizabethans*, Yale University Press, 1948, pp. 32–4.

Act I, Scene 4

1 SD **Mercutio** This name (from Brooke's *Romeus and Juliet*) suggests the mercurial qualities of Shakespeare's character, although it is etymologically unrelated to the Italian Mercurio. The original form in da Porto and Bandello is Marcuccio, an affectionate diminutive having approximately the value of 'cunning little Marco.'

1 SD **Torchbearers** In the Elizabethan production from which

the text of Q1 derives, these supernumeraries were apparently cut to a single Page. Similarly, the 'two or three' Servingmen of IV.2.1 SD and the 'three or four' of IV.4.13 SD are in each case cut to a single Servingman in Q1.

1 this speech It was the Elizabethan custom for a costumed messenger to deliver a speech introducing Maskers and apologizing for their joining a festivity without invitation. The Maskers have been discussing such a speech, which Benvolio rejects as prolix and out of date.

5 Tartar's painted bow This is the Roman or Cupid's bow, shaped like the line of the upper lip, as distinguished from the English bow, shaped like the segment of a circle.

7–8 ⟨Nor . . . entrance⟩ These two lines from Q1 are incorporated in the text of the present edition on the assumption that they stood in Shakespeare's foul papers but were overlooked by the Q2 compositor. Another theory is that Shakespeare added them to the promptbook version (represented by Q1) of his original text (represented by Q2). See H. R. Hoppe's edition of 1947, p. vi. The references to prologue and prompter harmonize with Shakespeare's habit of alluding to practices of the stage, and the trisyllabic *entrance* accords with similar pronunciations of *mistress* at II.3.194 and III.5.151.

12–21 heavy . . . bound Like the word-play of Sampson and Gregory (see I.1.1–11 N), Romeo's and Mercutio's puns and quibbles on *heavy* ('melancholy' and 'ponderous'), *light* (opposed to 'dark' and 'heavy'), *sole* and *soul*, *soar* and *sore*, and *bound* ('tied,' 'limit,' and 'leap') were considered witty in the 1590's. They are followed by bawdy quibbles on *burthen*, *thing*, *prick*, and *case* (ll. 23–9). There is a good deal more of the same in II.3.

37 proverb'd . . . phrase Romeo is thinking of some such proverb as 'A good candle-holder proves a good gamester,' since by looking on and not gambling he can lose nothing.

39 dun Editors usually emend Q2's *dum* to Q1's *done*, but since the variant spelling *dun* for 'done' does not appear in Q2, *dum* would appear to be the compositor's error for *dun*, 'dark.' Romeo, of course, is playing on *fair* and punning on 'done.'

41 Dun This was a quasi-proper name for any horse, whether or not actually a dun. The phrase 'Dun's in the mire,' meaning

135

'Things are at a standstill,' was the name of an indoor winter game in which a heavy log representing a horse stuck in the mud was hauled out by the players.

46–7 judgment . . . wits Judgment was one of the five inner or spiritual senses, as distinguished from the five outer or physical senses (here 'our five wits'). Mercutio means that the single mental faculty of judgment (which in quibbling about daylight Romeo neglects to use) can apprehend his intended meaning five times as well as can all five of the physical senses.

53, 54 Queen Mab, midwife The name *Mab* (which Ben Jonson uses for the Fairy Queen in his *Althorp Entertainment*) is probably a variant of Maeve, the heroic queen of Celtic legend. Mercutio calls her *midwife* (here pronounced 'middif') because she is that fairy who assists at the birth of men's dreams, 'the children of an idle brain, Begot of nothing but vain phantasy' (ll. 97–8).

55 agate stone That is, the tiny figure often carved in the agate set in a seal ring. Compare Falstaff on the diminutive size of his Page: 'I was never manned with an agate till now' (2 *Henry IV*, I.2.19).

57 atomi Editors usually follow the Q3 editor in emending Q2's *ottamie* to *atomies*, but Hoppe restores Q1's *atomi*, plural of Latin *atomus*, atom. (In Shakespeare's time the Latin plural *atomi* developed into the English singular *atomy*, atom, mote.) Q2's *ottamie* is evidently the compositor's misreading of *attomie* in Shakespeare's foul papers. Moreover, the variant forms in the two editions prove that the Q2 reading was not contaminated by Q1.

66 maid This Q1 reading would appear to be supported by Q2's *man*. Since the Q2 compositor occasionally misread *ie* as *n* and final *d* as *e*, *man* is apparently his misreading of *maid*. (Compare the compositor's misreading of *gaie* as *gan* at III.1.126, and of *exhald* as *exhale* at III.5.13.) It is possible, however, that *man* is a misreading of *maie*, 'may, maiden,' corrupted in Q1 to *maid*. For the latter suggestion the present editor is indebted to Mr. H. R. Hoppe.

78 suit That is, a petition to the monarch which will enable the courtier to extort a fee from the petitioner in return for interceding, or pretending to intercede, in his behalf.

94 carriage In Shakespeare's time pronunciation of the suffixes *-iage*, *-ion*, *-ial*, *-iar*, and *-ience* could be monosyllabic or disyllabic, depending on the metrical context. Disyllabic pronunciations of these suffixes (especially *-ion*) occur throughout *Romeo and Juliet*, but only one example of each is glossed: *carri-age* (I.4.94), *invocati-on* (II.1.27), *substanti-al* (II.1.183), *famili-ar* (III.3.6), and *pati-ence* (V.1.27). See Helge Kökeritz, *Shakespeare's Pronunciation*, Yale University Press, 1953, pp. 256, 293–4.

109–11 expire . . . death Romeo compares the length of his life to the term of a bond or mortgage for which his life itself is security. If the *consequence* of which he has a premonition brings the bond's term to a close, in default of payment he will have to forfeit his life.

114 SD They march . . . napkins The traditional scene division at this point accords with the modern custom of a curtain drop but obscures the continuity of action and fluidity of scene in an Elizabethan public playhouse, where the marching of the Maskers symbolizes a change of scene from the street outside Capulet's house to a hall within it. The Maskers retire to the back or sides of the forestage during the Servingmen's short scene (I.4.115–31), stepping forward at l. 131 when the dance party enters 'to' them.

115–31 Where 's Potpan . . . take all Editors usually assign these six speeches to three Servingmen, but there are actually four, in Q2 unconventionally numbered *Ser.*, *1.*, *2.*, and *3.*, rather than *1. Ser.*, *2.*, *3.*, and *4.* The present editor follows the numbering in Dowden's edition.

131 SD Enter . . . to the Maskers Since Capulet's feast is not a masquerade, masks are worn only by Romeo and his friends, the uninvited guests. See I.4.1 N and I.4.212–17 N.

194 goodman boy This is a double insult, since *goodman* was the title of a farmer or other person beneath the rank of gentleman but above that of laborer, and *boy* was used contemptuously of a green youngster, or one treated as such.

198 **set cock-a-hoop** This means literally, set the *cock* (spigot) on the *hoop* (of the barrel), thus letting the liquor flow freely. The same image for disorder appears at I.1.107 in the expression 'set abroach.'

200 SD **Aside** Capulet successively interrupts his quarrel with Tybalt in order to reply to a guest (l. 200), to compliment other guests (l. 203), to order his servants (l. 204), and to encourage the dancing (l. 205).

211–13 **the gentle sin . . . kiss** In atonement for the *rough* sin of profaning Juliet's hand by touching it with his own, Romeo proposes the *gentle sin* of kissing her hand.

212–17 **pilgrims . . . palmers** Although in da Porto's novella Romeo attends a Capelletti masquerade costumed as a nymph, in Shakespeare's play Capulet's feast is not a masquerade and Romeo is not costumed, as a pilgrim or otherwise. Shakespeare's conceit of Romeo as a pilgrim visiting the shrine of his love is suggested by the name Romeo itself, for in Italian it means literally 'Romer' or 'Rome-bound pilgrim.' In the Middle Ages the word was originally used in Palestine and elsewhere to designate pilgrims from Italy, but it ultimately grew to refer to a pilgrim's destination rather than his place of origin. In the *Vita Nuova* Dante distinguishes among the 'three separate denominations proper unto those who undertake journeys to the glory of God. They are called *Palmers* who go beyond the seas eastward [to Jerusalem], whence often they bring palm-branches. And *Pilgrims* [in addition to the general sense of "religious travelers"] . . . are they who journey unto the holy House of Gallicia; seeing that no other apostle was buried so far from his birth-place as was the blessed Saint James [Santiago de Compostela]. And there is a third sort who are called *Romers* [*romei*, plural of *romeo*]; in that they go . . . unto Rome.' (*La Vita Nuova*, XL, tr. D. G. Rossetti.)

224 **Thus . . . purg'd** It was not unusual for partners in an Elizabethan dance to kiss. Compare Ariel's song: 'Come unto these yellow sands, And then take hands. Curtsied when you have and kiss'd, The wild waves whist, Foot it featly here and there . . .' (*The Tempest*, I.2.375–9).

248 **Petruchio** Here and in *The Taming of the Shrew* Shakespeare spells the name Petruccio with a *ch* in order to retain the

soft Italian *c* in English. However, since the *i* in Petruccio is not vocalic, this English phonetic spelling results in the traditional mispronunciation 'Petruchi-o.'

262–75 Now old Desire . . . sweet According to Senecan tradition, this 'chorus' should precede rather than follow the act division. See Baldwin, *Shakspere's Five-Act Structure*, p. 744.

Act II, Scene 1

2 earth . . . center As everything on earth tends toward its center, so Romeo's body gravitates toward his heart, which has remained with Juliet.

4 He 's Here and at III.1.120, III.1.199, and III.5.39, the present editor prints the contracted form of Q2's *is;* and elsewhere the contracted forms of *am* (II.4.53), *are* (III.5.222), *would* (II.4.13), and *it* (II.1.222 and III.5.223).

7 Romeo . . . lover Since it was believed that a spirit could not speak until properly addressed, Mercutio in his parody of invocation follows the custom of reciting various names in the hope that the right one will cause the spirit to appear and speak. Hamlet does the same in addressing his father's ghost (*Hamlet*, I.4.44–5).

13 Abram An *Abram* or Abraham Man was 'one of a class of pretended lunatics who wandered over England seeking alms, after the dissolution of the religious houses' (OED); and thus the term became slang for a cheat or hypocrite. Since Cupid's blindness is misleading (considering his accuracy as an archer) and since he caused King Cophetua to fall in love with a beggar maid, Mercutio describes the god of love by reference to the typical Elizabethan hypocritical beggar. Editors have also explained *Abraham* (the reading of both Q2 and Q1) as alluding to the Old Testament Patriarch (*Abraham* in Hebrew meaning 'Father of Multitudes'), as a variant of *auburn* (i.e. 'auburn-haired'; see *Coriolanus*, II.3.21), and as an error for *Adam*, in allusion to the proverbial archer Adam Bell (see *Much Ado About Nothing*, I.1.260–1). For the editorial principle involved in the retention of this Q2 reading, see 'The Received Text,' pp. 18–19.

14 King Cophetua This hero of a popular Elizabethan ballad fell in love with and married a wandering beggar girl named Penelophon—or Zenelophon, as the name appears in *Love's*

Labour's Lost (IV.1.67). On Cophetua's first sight of Penelophon, Cupid, 'The blinded boy, that shoots so trim, From heaven down did hie; He drew a dart and shot at him, In place where he did lie.' (Thomas Percy, *Reliques of Ancient English Poetry*, ed. 1839, vol. *1*, bk. II, no. 6.)

38 open-arse Q1's *Et cætera* (euphemistic for 'pudendum') is the traditional reading here, but in adopting it editors usually suppress Q2's *or* and fail to recognize that if l. 38 is to scan properly the word omitted after Q2's *open* must be a monosyllable. Thus the metrical as well as the semantic context requires the reading *open-arse*, an old name for the medlar tree or 'that kind of fruit As maids call medlars when they laugh alone' (ll. 35–6). Chaucer's Reeve uses it in referring to the fact that the medlar is not worth eating until overripe and slightly decayed: 'This white top writeth myne olde yeris; Myn herte is also mowled [mouldy] as myne heris, But if [unless] I fare as dooth an *open-ers*.' ('The Reeve's Prologue,' in *The Poetical Works of Chaucer*, ed. F. N. Robinson, Boston, 1933, p. 66.) For the editorial principle involved in this emendation, see 'The Received Text,' pp. 20–1.

38 pop'rin pear The *poppering pear* was so called after its place of origin, the town of Poperinghe in Flanders. Mercutio here couples it with *open-arse* to indicate two different varieties of the same essential kind, Romeo and Rosaline. There may also be a quibble on 'phallus'; see Kökeritz, *Shakespeare's Pronunciation*, pp. 136–8.

43 Romeo Here the traditional scene division again obscures the Elizabethan fluidity of scene and continuity of action, emphasized by the rhyme of *wound* with *found*. Romeo, who is usually visible to the audience during Mercutio's raillery (ll. 7–39), now comes forward from his hiding place, and the scene of the forestage changes from a street outside the wall to the orchard within it.

51 SD Enter . . . window Editors usually follow Capell (1768) in locating this entrance (omitted from Q2 and Q1) after II.1.43. However, since the light at the window is the twilight glow of dawn (the East) and since Juliet herself is the sun, its imminent rising designates in metaphor her anticipated appearance at the window. Only after Romeo has invoked the sun to rise (l. 46) and to cast off Diana's livery (l. 51) does the 'sun' actually 'rise': Juliet enters at the window, causing Romeo's triple exclamation of delight at first catching sight of his beloved (ll. 52–3). Thus Romeo's 'invocation' is Shakespeare's preparation for an effective entrance by Juliet, an ironic echo of Mercutio's parody of invocation in the immediately preceding lines, and a transitional device functioning as a buffer between Mercutio's ribaldry in the first part of II.1 and Juliet's 'true-love passion' (l. 146) in the latter part of that scene. See Richard Hosley, 'Juliet's Entrance,' *The Times Literary Supplement*, May 22, 1953, p. 333.

51 SD **window** Although in a proscenium-arch theater Juliet usually here enters on a 'balcony,' in an Elizabethan public playhouse she enters on the upper stage, representing her window. Compare the Q1 and Q2 directions at III.5.1. For structural details of the upper stage, rear stage, and forestage in various Elizabethan public theaters, see C. Walter Hodges, *The Globe Restored*, London, 1953.

59 **spheres** In medieval and Renaissance astronomy the erratic motions of the planets (and of the moon) were explained according to the Ptolemaic system, in which each planet is carried about the earth by a hollow crystalline sphere concentric with the earth. The general notion persisted a century or more after publication of the Copernican hypothesis (1543).

73 **puffing** Editors usually emend Q2's *puffing* to Q1's *pacing*, but the Q2 reading apparently alludes to the personification of winds in old maps as cloud-shaped heads puffing air from distended cheeks. It is possible, however, that *puffing* is the Q2 compositor's misreading of *passing*, Hoppe's emendation. For discussion of the three readings see Duthie, 'The Text of Shakespeare's *Romeo and Juliet*,' pp. 24–6, and Hosley, 'The Received Text,' p. 19 and n. 23.

82–4 **What's Montague . . . a man** Editors usually correct these lines by conflating them with the variant Q1 text, but since it is not entirely clear that Q2 is corrupt, the present editor follows Hoppe in reprinting the text as it stands in Q2.

159 **contract** Juliet uses this legal term because according to Elizabethan law the lovers have entered into a formal betrothal

contract. Such a betrothal was often legally binding as a marriage, although it did not morally license consummation of the marriage until a member of the clergy had performed the nuptial ceremony (compare II.5.36–7). See Davis P. Harding, 'Elizabethan Betrothals and *Measure for Measure*,' *The Journal of English and Germanic Philology*, *49* (1950), 149–50.

209 **dear** Hoppe here restores Q2's *Neece*. However, except for the OED's one doubtful example from around 1470, there is no record of the word 'niece' used as a form of address to an unrelated woman; and the independent emendations of both the F2 editor (to *sweete*) and the Q4 editor (to *Deere*) show that the Q2 reading was considered corrupt in the early 17th century. Since *c* was a common compositor's error for *r*, it seems likely that the Q2 compositor misread *deere* as *Neece*. For Q2's *My Neece* Q1 has *Madame*.

222 **silken threed** The Q2 spelling *threed* indicates a common Elizabethan pronunciation of 'thread.' This pronunciation in turn suggests that *threed* is stressed, that *plucks it* is monosyllabic, and that Q1's monosyllabic variant *silke* (the traditional reading) is an error for *silken*.

226–9 **Good night . . . rest** Editors here follow the Q4 editor and Pope (1723) in printing the Q1 assignment of ll. 226–7 to Juliet and of ll. 228–9 to Romeo. However, in view of the Q1 reporter's recurrent errors of speech assignment (see H. R. Hoppe, *The Bad Quarto of Romeo and Juliet*, Cornell University Press, 1948, pp. 125–6), the present editor reprints the text as it stands in Q2, with the addition from Q3 of Romeo's omitted speech heading to the second half of l. 226 and the shift of his heading at l. 229 to l. 230. For a detailed account of the Q1 and Q2 errors here involved, see 'The Received Text,' pp. 26–8; Clifford Leech, 'Notes on . . . the Received Text of *Romeo and Juliet*,' *Shakespeare Quarterly*, *5* (1954), 94–5; and Richard Hosley, 'The "Good Night, Good Night" Sequence in *Romeo and Juliet*,' *ibid*., pp. 96–8.

230–3 **The grey-ey'd Morn . . . wheels** These four lines constitute Shakespeare's revision of an original version, which he failed to delete from his manuscript and which was therefore set up by the Q2 compositor as a duplication of the revision (see Appendix A). Since 1723 editors have followed Pope and the Q4 editor in deleting the original version from Romeo's speech in II.1 and in assigning the revised version to the Friar at the beginning of II.2. However, since the original version stands in Romeo's speech two lines before the end of II.1, the passage would appear to belong to him; and the present editor follows the F2 editor and Rowe (1709) in assigning it to Romeo. The image of the 'grey-ey'd Morn' is echoed by Romeo at III.5.19 ('I'll say yon grey is not the Morning's eye'); and the imagery of the passage is generally akin both to that used by Romeo at II.1.45–6 and III.5.7–10 and by other characters apropos of Romeo at I.1.121–2, I.1.137–9, and III.2.1–25; whereas the Friar never elsewhere alludes to classical mythology or personifies Day or Night or their aspects in the Homeric manner. The Q1 assignment of the passage to the Friar is apparently the reporter's memorial error. For detailed discussion of this 'revisional duplication' and of others at III.3.40–3, IV.1.111–12, and V.3.108–20, see 'The Received Text,' pp. 28–32. Duplications of a single word or phrase are listed in the note to V.3.102.

231 **Check'ring** This Q1 reading suggests that Q2's *Checking* in the revised Q2 version of the 'grey-ey'd Morn' passage is a misprint for *Checkring*, the reading of the original Q2 version.

Act II, Scene 2

18 SD **Enter Romeo** Editors occasionally follow Pope in locating this entrance after l. 26, but the location of the entrance in Q2 is a calculated irony: Romeo, who is to be the victim of *Poison*, enters just before the word is mentioned (l. 20) and overhears the Friar's homily on *Grace* and *rude Will*.

29, 36 **distemper'd, distemp'rature** Both words suggest the idea of mental disturbance as a result of the four bodily humors being disproportionately mixed or tempered.

Act II, Scene 3

4–6 **Why . . . run mad** Editors usually follow Q2 in arranging this prose passage and that at III.1.1–2 as verse, but in each case Q2 appears to have been contaminated by the erroneous arrangement in Q1. See 'The Received Text,' pp. 23–4.

21 **Prince of Cats** Tybalt or Tibert (Tebaldo in da Porto and Bandello) is the name of the cat in the medieval French cycle of

animal satires concerning Reynard the Fox. In III.1 Mercutio repeats his joke by calling Tybalt 'ratcatcher' (l. 76) and 'King of Cats' (l. 78).

25 butcher . . . button Tybalt is such an accurate fencer that he can pink any button he chooses on his opponent's jacket.

27 first and second cause These were, according to the code of the duello, two of the various grounds for a gentleman's recognizing an affront to his honor and therefore challenging the offender to a duel. (Compare Mercutio's use of the phrase in the Q1 version of his death-speech, p. 160.) See Touchstone's satire on such quarreling in *As You Like It* (V.4.48–108), and compare Armado's complaints against Cupid: 'The first and second cause will not serve my turn; the passado he respects not, the duello he regards not. His disgrace is to be called boy, but his glory is to subdue men' (*Love's Labour's Lost*, I.2.184–8). Compare also Peter's quarreling with the Musicians (IV.4.141–54).

28 passado . . . hai The *passado* (Italian *passata*, 'pass,' 'thrust') is a lunging thrust involving the passing of one foot before the other while delivering the attack. The *punto reverso* (Italian *punta reversa*, 'point reversed') is a back-handed thrust delivered from the left side of the attacker's body. The word *hai* (Italian, 'thou hast [it]') means a home thrust or death blow. See Horace S. Craig, 'Dueling Scenes and Terms in Shakespeare's Plays,' *University of California Publications in English, 9* (1940), 1–28. Craig also discusses the medieval long sword, and distinguishes between the rapier-and-dagger swordplay of the young gallants and the sword-and-buckler swashbuckling of the servants.

37 bones Mercutio derides the fashion-mongers because the old seats are too hard for their bones, which are presumably afflicted with syphilis—'the Neapolitan bone-ache . . . the curse dependent on those that war for a placket' (*Troilus and Cressida*, II.3.20–2). There may also be a pun on French 'bons,' since the *pardon-me's* affectedly interlard their speech with foreign expressions.

76 wild goose chase This is a horse race in which the rider who can seize the lead must be followed cross-country wherever he goes.

106 occupy This word's sense of 'copulate' is alluded to by Doll Tearsheet: 'God's light! these villains will make the word [captain] as odious as the word "occupy," which was an excellent good word before it was ill sorted' (2 *Henry IV*, II.4.160–2).

107 SD Enter . . . Man Editors usually follow Q2 in locating this direction after 'Here's goodly gear' (l. 108), but the Q2 location would appear to be due to the compositor's having reproduced the erroneous location in Q1. The present editor follows the location in F1. See 'The Received Text,' pp. 21–2.

112 fan It was the extreme of fashion for a lady to use a fan so large that a servant was required to carry it.

146 'Lady, lady' Mercutio quotes from the refrain of a popular ballad on Susanna and the Elders: 'A woman fair and virtuous: Lady, lady, Why should we not of her learn thus To live godly?' Compare Sir Toby Belch: 'Tilly-vally, lady! "There dwelt a man in Babylon, lady, lady!"' (*Twelfth Night*, II.3.83–4).

182 Bid . . . afternoon Editors usually print 'Bid her devise' as a separate dimeter line, but the line as it stands in Q2 appears to be a fourteener. There is another fourteener at II.4.15.

Act II, Scene 4

25 jaunce This may be the Q2 compositor's misreading of 'jaunte' or a colloquial development from the plural form 'jaunts.'

Act III, Scene 1

75 Alla stoccatho Editors usually emend Q2's *Alla stucatho* to *Alla stoccata*, an Italian fencing term meaning 'at the thrust,' the *stoccata* (from 'stocco,' rapier) being a thrust delivered with the fingernails up. However, since *stoccado* was a common Elizabethan variant of *stoccata*, Q1's *Allastockado* preserves essentially the correct reading, for Q2's *stucatho* (or *stocatho*, misread by the compositor) would appear to reproduce Shakespeare's phonetic spelling of *stoccado*, the *th* being an attempt to render the Spanish fricative *d*, as in *renegatho* (*Twelfth Night*, III.2.74). Compare Shallow's *stoccadoes* in *The Merry Wives of Windsor* (II.1.234). Mercutio uses the expression figuratively for Tybalt's blustering.

126 He gay Editors usually emend Q2's *He gan* to Q1's 'A liue' (i.e. alive), but the present editor follows Hoppe in interpreting *gan* as the Q2 compositor's misreading of *gaie*, a variant spelling of *gay*. Compare the compositor's error two lines later of *end* for *eied* (III.1.128).

141 **Citizens** Editors usually interpret Q2's *Citti.* as designating a single Citizen (as at l. 143), but ll. 141–2 would appear to be spoken by two different Citizens. Compare I.1.76 N.

165–6 **one hand . . . the other** The swordplay here described is of the sword-and-dagger variety, in which the left hand, holding a dagger or wearing a mailed gauntlet, parries the attack and the right hand thrusts with the rapier. See II.3.28 N.

188 **Montague** This traditional emendation of the Q2 speech heading *Capulet* was first made by the Q4 editor. Hoppe restores the Q2 reading, but the passage in question (ll. 188–90) seems dramatically more appropriate to Montague and its assignment to him has the theatrical advantage of giving one of Romeo's parents something to say in a scene where they would otherwise remain mute.

201 **Mercy . . . kill** The unwiseness of a clement civil policy is discussed by Machiavelli, who writes that a prince 'must not mind incurring the charge of cruelty for the purpose of keeping his subjects united and faithful; for, with a very few examples, he will be more merciful than those who, from excess of tenderness, allow disorders to arise, from whence spring bloodshed and rapine; for these as a rule injure the whole community, while the executions carried out by the prince injure only individuals.' (*The Prince*, ch. 17, Modern Library ed., p. 60.) Compare I.1.99–100 N.

Act III, Scene 2

1–31 **Gallop apace . . . wear them** This passage is occasionally called Juliet's serenade or evening song.

3 **Phaeton** The son of Phoebus Apollo, Phaeton was permitted by his father to drive the chariot of the sun. However, he was unable to control the horses, which ran away with him, drawing the sun so close to the earth as to dry up large areas which are now the great deserts. To prevent the universe from being destroyed, Jupiter was forced to kill Phaeton with a thunderbolt. See Ovid, *Metamorphoses*, II.1–328 (Loeb ed.)

6 **runaway** The meaning is not clear. If *runaway* alludes to the Phaeton myth, it probably designates the sun, which Juliet wishes would move faster (as when it ran away with Phaeton) so as to bring in night earlier than usual. This interpretation is supported

by Lorenzo's use of the word: 'But come at once; For the close night doth play the *runaway*, And we are stay'd for at Bassanio's feast' (*The Merchant of Venice*, II.6.46–8).

31 SD Enter Nurse with cords In place of this direction Q1 has 'Enter Nurse wringing her hands, with the ladder of cords in her lap.' Presumably in the production on which the Q1 text is based the Nurse was here 'discovered' seated in the rear stage. In Q1 Juliet's serenade is cut to four lines, and the Q2 phrase 'O here comes my Nurse' is omitted.

47 cockatrice The *cockatrice* or basilisk was a fabulous serpent whose glance was supposed to be fatal. Compare Sir Toby Belch: 'This will so fright them both [Cesario and Sir Andrew Aguecheek] that they will kill one another by the look, like *cockatrices*' (*Twelfth Night*, III.4.214–15).

87 forsworn, all Editors usually correct Q2's long and awkward line 'All perjur'd, all forsworn, all naught, all dissemblers' by rearranging the lineation of ll. 86–7. However, the present editor retains the Q2 lineation and omits the phrase 'all naught' as a first thought which Shakespeare had neglected to delete from his foul papers. See V.3.102 N.

Act III, Scene 3

1 SD Enter Friar Q1's separate entrances for the Friar and Romeo accord with the Q2 text and apparently reflect the bookkeeper's correction (in the promptbook) of the original direction in Shakespeare's foul papers, 'Enter Friar and Romeo.' In an Elizabethan public theater the Friar and Romeo enter 'at several doors' on the forestage, representing the Friar's cell. Compare V.2.1 SD N.

166–7 Either be gone . . . hence That is, be gone from hence, disguised, either before the watch be set or (at the latest) by the break of day.

Act III, Scene 4

12 desp'rate tender Capulet's negotiation for a marriage de convenance without his daughter's consent reflects the strict parental authority exercised by Elizabethans in arranging marriages for their children. (See Charles T. Prouty, *The Sources of Much Ado*

About Nothing, Yale University Press, 1950, pp. 44–5.) Such authority helps to explain Capulet's anger in III.5, where Juliet, who of course cannot marry Paris because she is already married to Romeo, seems to Capulet to be rejecting a 'good' match out of sheer wilfulness. On the concern of fathers for their daughters' marriages, compare Leonato in *Much Ado About Nothing,* Polonius in *Hamlet,* Brabantio in *Othello,* and Prospero in *The Tempest.*

Act III, Scene 5

1–36 Wilt thou be gone . . . dark our woes These lines compose an aubade or dawn song, a traditional verse form of the troubadours celebrating the hour of parting between two lovers at dawn. As here, the aubade is often a duet in which the lovers debate whether dawn is actually at hand. As an example of Shakespeare's functional use of a conventional verse form, Romeo and Juliet's aubade may be compared with their sonnet at I.4.210–23.

13 exhal'd Editors usually emend Q2's *exhale* to Q1's *exhales,* but the Q2 reading would appear to be the compositor's error for *exhald.* For a list of the Q2 compositor's recurrent misreadings of final *d* as *e,* see 'The Received Text,' p. 20, n. 27.

31 Some say . . . eyes Because the beautiful-voiced lark has ugly eyes, whereas the croaking toad has beautiful ones.

36 SD Nurse The Q2 direction 'Enter Madam and Nurse' probably stood in Shakespeare's foul papers as a marginal direction, 'Enter Nurse. Madam'—that is, Enter the Nurse, calling 'Madam'; and accordingly the direction was amplified to 'Enter Madam and Nurse' and duplicated in the text as '*Nur.* Madam.' See Sir Walter Greg, *The Editorial Problem in Shakespeare,* Oxford, 1942, p. 61, n. 2.

37–40 Madam . . . look about In a proscenium-arch theater the Nurse usually delivers the warning from offstage. But in the Elizabethan production represented by Q1, it was apparently shifted to l. 59 in order to 'cover' Juliet's descent from the upper stage. In such a method of staging the Nurse enters on the forestage. See III.5.67 SD N.

62 renowm'd This Q2 spelling indicates an Elizabethan pro-

148

nunciation emphasizing the etymology of 'renown,' from Old French *renomer*.

67 SD ⟨She goeth down from the window⟩ This Q1 stage direction indicates that in an Elizabethan public playhouse Juliet here descends from the upper to the lower stage by means of the tiring-house stairs, and thus that the balance of III.5 is played on the lower rather than the upper level. The text in Q2 and the present edition reproduces the original version of Shakespeare's foul papers. After the Wife's entrance and speech at l. 64, Juliet expresses her surprise in soliloquy (ll. 65–7), exits from the upper stage after l. 67, descends to the lower level, and re-enters 'to' the Wife on the rear stage or the forestage; at which point the scene of the lower stage (having changed on the Wife's entrance from orchard to house) changes from a location outside Juliet's bedroom to one inside it. However, Shakespeare's original version is unstageworthy in that it involves a pause in the action of eight or ten seconds during Juliet's descent. The text in Q1, on the other hand, in part reflects the promptbook version of the staging. In that edition the Nurse's warning is shifted from its Q2 position at III.5.37–40 to l. 59, and Juliet's soliloquies at ll. 60–4 and 65–7 are eliminated. Thus Juliet begins her descent simultaneously with Romeo's exit at l. 59, the descent being 'covered' by the dialogue and stage business of the Nurse's and the Wife's calling Juliet and knocking at her door. At l. 67 Juliet re-enters to the Wife and Nurse on the rear stage or the forestage, where the action proceeds. (If she enters on the rear stage, the players must subsequently 'flow out' to the forestage in order to play the 'upbraiding' scene with Capulet.) In Otway's restoration version entitled *The History and Fall of Caius Marius*, this staging problem was solved by representing a garden scene (see Hazelton Spencer, *Shakespeare Improved*, Harvard University Press, 1927, p. 295); and in the 18th century Romeo and Juliet were 'brought in *tète à tète* [*sic*] on the platform of the stage' (from a contemporary account cited by A. C. Sprague, *Shakespeare and the Actors*, Harvard University Press, 1944, p. 308). In a modern proscenium-arch theater, the problem posed by this transition of scene is usually solved by representing the interior rather than the exterior of Juliet's bed-

room, which the Wife enters by a door at l. 67 after Romeo has left by the window at l. 42. In this method of staging, the Q2 text requires no alteration. For a more detailed account, see Richard Hosley, 'The Use of the Upper Stage in *Romeo and Juliet*,' *Shakespeare Quarterly*, 5 (1954).

172, 173 **Capulet, Nurse** The present editor here follows the traditional assignment of speeches, based on the corrections of the Q4 editor and Capell (1768). In Q2 Capulet's 'O—Godigoden!' (l. 172) and the Nurse's 'May not one speak?' (l. 173) are printed on separate lines without speech headings, and the reading *Father* stands as part of the 'text proper' immediately before 'O—Godigoden!' That *Father* is an error for the speech heading *Fa.* (used regularly for Capulet from l. 161 to his exit) is corroborated by the Q1 assignment of 'O—Godigoden!' to Capulet, it being clear from variations in text and spelling that Q2 was not here contaminated by Q1. If the Nurse's heading was missing from Shakespeare's foul papers, the Q2 compositor may have misinterpreted Capulet's heading as text in order to set right the sequence of speech headings.

176 **Day, night—work, play** For this reading Q2 has 'Day, night, hour, tide, time, work, play.' Some editors reprint the Q2 text verbatim and others conflate it with the variant text of Q1, but Hoppe's deletion of 'hour, tide, time' provides a good reading with a minimum of alteration and accords with the metrical pattern. Since Shakespeare's foul papers had probably been messily rewritten at this point, the text may well be corrupt beyond editorial redemption.

180 **limb'd** Editors usually emend Q2's *liand* to Q1's *trainde*, but the Q2 reading would appear to be the compositor's misreading of *limd*. Compare the Q2 spelling *lims* for 'limbs' at II.2.34 and V.3.36. For some of the Q2 compositor's recurrent misreadings of words with minim letters, see 'The Received Text,' p. 20, n. 28.

Act IV, Scene 1

38 **evening mass** During the Middle Ages the mass was occasionally performed in the afternoon or evening, and the custom, although prohibited in the 16th century, lingered on in some localities long after the Renaissance.

57 **label** This was a strip of ribbon or parchment attached to the bottom of a deed or other legal document. There was a separate label for each party to the agreement, who impressed his seal in a ball of soft wax enclosing the lower end of the label.

63 **umpeer** This Q2 spelling indicates an Elizabethan pronunciation emphasizing the etymology of 'umpire,' from Middle English *noumpere* and Old French *nompere* (modern *non-pair*, 'peerless, nonpareil'). (The *n* of *noumpere* was transferred to the indefinite article by the same process of 'separation' whereby *a naddre* became *an addre*, 'an adder.')

81 **charnel house** This was a vault or shed attached to the church in which were deposited the bones tossed up in the common practice of digging new graves on the site of old. Compare *Hamlet*, V.1.

100 **wanny** Editors usually emend Q2's *many* to F2's *mealy* or Q4's *paly*, but the present editor follows Hoppe in interpreting *many* as the Q2 compositor's misreading of *wany*, an Elizabethan spelling variant of *wanny*.

105 **two and forty hours** Shakespeare may have derived this figure for the duration of Juliet's sleep from Painter's novella, where it is described as 'forty hours at the least.' However, forty-two hours cannot be interpreted literally, being too long a period to allow Juliet to awaken early Thursday morning and too short for Friday. The most satisfactory time scheme of the play dates the beginning of the action Sunday morning. Capulet's feast is held Sunday night (I.4), and Romeo and Juliet part at dawn on Monday (II.1). During Monday the lovers are married (II.5) and Mercutio and Tybalt are killed (III.1). The lovers spend Monday night together, and on Tuesday at dawn Romeo departs for Mantua (III.5). During Tuesday Juliet obtains the potion from the Friar (IV.1) and Capulet enthusiastically advances the marriage from Thursday to Wednesday (IV.2). Tuesday night (a day ahead of the Friar's plan) Juliet drinks the potion (IV.3) and Wednesday morning is discovered apparently dead (IV.4). Late Wednesday afternoon Balthasar notifies Romeo of Juliet's death (V.1), and Romeo returns to Verona that same evening, arriving at the tomb after midnight Wednesday (V.3). Thus the action ends early Thursday morning, Juliet apparently having slept somewhat over twenty-four hours.

Act IV, Scene 2

37 SD Exeunt ⟨Nurse and Juliet⟩ Act IV illustrates the possibilities in an Elizabethan public playhouse of rapidly alternating the action between forestage and rear stage. At IV.2.37 Juliet and the Nurse exit from the forestage, to be discovered a moment later on the rear stage at the beginning of IV.3. During the potion scene (IV.3) Juliet comes out on the forestage to talk with the Wife and to deliver the potion speech, but at the end of the scene she retires to the rear stage and 'falls upon her bed within the curtains,' which are then closed so that the scene of domestic preparation may be played on the forestage (IV.4.1–28). At IV.4.29 the Nurse opens the curtains of the rear stage, where Juliet is discovered apparently dead (see IV.4.29 N). The lamentation scene (IV.4.29–175) is then played on the forestage. For an argument that the potion scene and the lamentation scene cannot be played upon the upper stage, see 'The Use of the Upper Stage in *Romeo and Juliet.*'

Act IV, Scene 3

47 mandrakes The *mandrake* or *mandragora* is a plant with opiate properties (see *Othello*, III.3.330), the root of which is often forked so as to resemble the legs of a human being. It had fabulous virtues in magic and medicine, and when pulled from the earth was supposed to shriek and cause hearers to go mad or die. For this reason dogs were supposedly harnessed to draw it from the ground.

Act IV, Scene 4

13 hood This would appear to be a variant spelling of 'hud' (cover, shell, husk), used metaphorically in the sense of 'an empty person.' Compare the Q2 spelling *hudwinckt* for 'hoodwink'd' at I.4.4. Some editors, interpreting *hood* as the suffix indicating generality as in 'womanhood,' hyphenate *jealous hood* and gloss it as 'jealousy,' the abstract for the concrete.

17 Peter In Q1 this name appears as *Will*, presumably because Will Kemp had played the part of Peter (see IV.4.129 N). The present editor is indebted to Mr. Cyrus Hoy for calling his attention to this variant.

29 **Nurse** At this point the traditional scene division again obscures the continuity of action and fluidity of scene in an Elizabethan public theater, and has induced editors to direct the Nurse offstage at IV.4.28, only to re-enter immediately at l. 29. The Nurse, however, remains on the forestage and after Capulet's exit at l. 28 opens the curtains of the rear stage, where Juliet is discovered lying on her bed; and thus the scene of the forestage changes from a location outside Juliet's bedroom to one (in conjunction with the rear stage) inside it. For a more detailed account, see 'The Use of the Upper Stage in *Romeo and Juliet*.'

34 **set up his rest** This expression, from the card game of primero, means literally 'staked his reserve.' There is probably also a pun on 'wrest,' wresting instrument, tuning key. See Kökeritz, *Shakespeare's Pronunciation*, p. 140.

107 **rosemary** Being an evergreen, rosemary symbolizes remembrance and was accordingly used at both weddings and funerals. See Philip Williams, 'The Rosemary Theme in *Romeo and Juliet*,' *Modern Language Notes*, *68* (1953), 400–3. Compare II.3.209 and IV.4.123 SD.

123 SD **They all . . . Musicians** Editors usually follow the Q4 editor in directing the Musicians to enter with Paris and the Friar at IV.4.60. However, the Q1 directions at l. 123 support the evidence of Q2, where *Exeunt* is apparently designed for Capulet, the Wife, Paris, and the Friar, but the singular *manet* for the Nurse, indicating that she is the only actor to remain on stage at IV.4.123 and thus that the Musicians do not enter until this point. See Richard Hosley, 'A Stage Direction in *Romeo and Juliet*,' *The Times Literary Supplement*, June 13, 1952, p. 391.

129 SD **Peter** The reading of Q2 indicates that the role of Peter was probably played by Will Kemp, the famous comic actor of Shakespeare's company. The name 'Will' is also used for Peter in Q1 (see IV.4.17 N). From speech headings in *Much Ado About Nothing* it appears that Kemp also played the part of Dogberry.

135 **'My Heart is Full'** Editors usually follow the Q4 editor in emending this Q2 reading to 'My heart is full of woe,' which has

been identified as a line from the anonymous song 'A Pleasant New Ballad of Two Lovers.' This emendation may be correct, but it has the appearance of a sophistication by the Q4 editor. The present editor reprints the substance of the Q2 text and punctuation, interpreting 'My Heart is Full' as the name of the tune (real or imaginary) which Peter's 'heart itself' is playing. That is, to 'comfort' him, Peter wishes the Musicians to play 'Heart's Ease,' a 'merry dump' which will counteract his heart's sorrowful tune. Peter's use of the term 'dump' is of course a malapropism.

148-9 **re . . . fa you** With *re* Peter quibbles on 'ray' (beray, befoul) and with *fa* on 'fay' (cleanse, polish). In this context 'ray' and 'fay' probably also mean 'to beat.' See Kökeritz, *Shakespeare's Pronunciation*, pp. 105-6.

155-7 **When . . . sound** These lines are from 'In Commendation of Music,' a song by Richard Edwards printed in a popular Elizabethan miscellany, *The Paradise of Dainty Devices* (1576).

Act V, Scene 1

15 **fares my Juliet** The Q2 reading 'How doth my Lady Juliet' would appear to involve the compositor's duplication of part of the immediately preceding line, 'How doth my Lady'; and if so, Q1, in here reading 'How fares my Juliet,' probably preserves the text of Shakespeare's foul papers. See Sir Walter Greg, *Principles of Emendation in Shakespeare*, British Academy Shakespeare Lecture, London, 1928, p. 52, n. 28.

24 **in** This Q2 spelling indicates an unstressed Elizabethan pronunciation of 'e'en.'

Act V, Scene 2

1 SD **Enter Friar John** This Q1 direction and the Q2 dialogue of ll. 1-3 suggest that Q2's 'Enter Lawrence' after l. 1 is the book-keeper's correction in Shakespeare's foul papers of the original direction before l. 1, 'Enter Friar John to Friar Lawrence.' The book-keeper, however, apparently did not delete the last three words of the original direction. In an Elizabethan public playhouse John and Lawrence enter 'severally' on the forestage, representing the Friar's cell. Compare III.3.1 SD N.

6 **associate** It was generally required that a friar should not travel unless accompanied by a fellow-member of his order.

11 **Seal'd up the doors** This was a frequent occurrence during the London plagues of Shakespeare's time.

Act V, Scene 3

21 SD **Balthasar** The erroneous Q2 designation of Romeo's servant as Peter may be due to the servant's being so named in *Romeus and Juliet* (ultimately after the Italian Pietro, Juliet's servant in da Porto but Romeo's in Bandello), or to Will Kemp's doubling in the parts of Balthasar and the Nurse's servant Peter, whose character is Shakespeare's invention. See IV.4.129 SD N.

102 **shall I believe** The Q2 phrase 'I will believe' is omitted from the present edition as a first thought which had not been deleted from Shakespeare's foul papers and which was therefore printed in Q2 immediately before its revision, 'Shall I believe.' Other short undeleted first thoughts omitted from the present edition are *did* (I.4.212), *Cozen* (III.1.151), *And* (III.2.9), *Rauenous* (III.2.76), *all naught* (III.2.87), and *O* (V.3.191). See 'The Received Text,' p. 28 and n. 43.

107 **pallet** Editors usually follow the Q3 editor in emending Q2's *pallat* to *pallace*. However, the Q2 reading is a common Elizabethan spelling variant of *pallet*, an image which supports the theme that Juliet's wedding bed is indeed her grave. Compare I.4.252, III.5.140, IV.4.64 and V.3.28.

187 SD **Citizens** This addition to Q2's direction 'Enter Prince' is suggested both by Q1's 'with others' and by the Wife's reference in Q2 to people running toward the monument (ll. 191–3). Moreover, the appearance of the Citizens at this point has a symbolic value which rounds out the theme of civil disorder. Here and at III.1.144 the Prince is presumably attended by the Train mentioned at I.1.83 SD.

189 SD **Enter Capels** In Q2 this stage direction is duplicated after l. 201 as 'Enter Capulet and his Wife.' The first direction is presumably the book-keeper's correction of the second, Shakespeare's erroneously located original direction.

216 **Seal up** G. B. Harrison suggests that at this point the curtains of the rear stage are closed to conceal the three bodies

NOTES

(*Shakespeare: Major Plays and the Sonnets,* New York, 1948). In the modern theater such concealment is unnecessary, since at this point the play is usually cut to its closing speeches, around V.3.291.

297 **jointure** This is the marriage portion or dowry settled on a bride by the bridegroom's family against the event of her husband's prior decease.

299 **ray** Editors usually emend Q2's *raie* to *raise,* the reading of Brooke's *Romeus and Juliet,* which in turn would seem to be supported by Q1's *erect.* However, since Romeo's statue is to 'lie' by the side of Juliet's (l. 303), it is clear that in Shakespeare's play the proposed 'statues' are high relief figures on sarcophagi.

APPENDIX A
Text and Date

The most authoritative source of the text of *Romeo and Juliet* is the 'good' Second Quarto, printed 'by Thomas Creede for Cuthbert Burby' in 1599.[1] That the copy consisted mainly of Shakespeare's 'foul papers' (working manuscript) is in part suggested by the inconsistent designation of characters in speech headings, for it seems likely that a character's dramatic function rather than his proper name would occasionally suggest itself to the author as he wrote out his manuscript.[2] Capulet's Wife, for example, is designated by such various speech headings as Wife, Mother, Old Lady, and Lady; and on the two occasions when Capulet speaks to Juliet his normal heading changes to Father. In a promptbook, on the other hand, such irregularities of designation would necessarily have been normalized in order to simplify the book-keeper's task of regulating performances. Additional evidence that Shakespeare's foul papers served as copy for Q2 is provided by a number of duplicate versions of individual words, phrases, and passages throughout the 'text proper' of the play. In each case one version appears to be the author's revision of the other, which he had not (or had not clearly) deleted from his manuscript and which was therefore set up along with its revision by the Q2 compositor. An example of 'revisional duplication' is the phrase 'I will believe,' printed in Q2 immediately before the 'Shall I believe' which the context demands and which editors customarily print as the revision, after deleting Shakespeare's first thought (V.3.102). Since the book-keeper or his scribe would recognize such duplications as stigmata of the author's composition, it is unlikely that the revisional duplications would have been reproduced in the promptbook.[3] Another kind of Q2 duplication, chiefly in stage directions but also in speech headings, suggests that the book-keeper, in preparation for transcribing the promptbook, had looked over Shakespeare's foul papers and added to them occasional notes clarifying the location of entrances and the designation of characters, without however deleting Shakespeare's original notation. Examples are afforded by the duplication of directions for the Friar's entrance at the beginning of V. 2, and by the speech heading 'M. Wife. 2.' at I.1.83. Thus the copy for Q2 appears to have been a text of *Romeo and Juliet* from which the promptbook was subsequently derived, either by direct transcription of the foul papers or by transcription of a 'fair copy' itself transcribed from the foul papers. The statement on the title page of Q2 that the text in that edition is 'newly corrected, augmented, and amended' does not mean that Q2 is the revision of an earlier version of *Romeo and Juliet* but rather that the authentic text is now being published to replace the pirated edition of 1597. The title page of Q2 also records that *Romeo and Juliet* had been 'sundry times publicly acted by the right Honorable the Lord Chamberlain his Servants.' Neither Q2 nor the 1597 Quarto was entered in the Stationers' Register.

The debased state of the text in the 'bad' First Quarto of *Romeo and Juliet*, printed 'by John Danter' in 1597,[4] suggests that this edition is one of the 'stolen and surreptitious copies' mentioned by Heminge and Condell in their epistle to the reader of the First Folio (1623). Although in the 18th century Q1 was thought to be an early draft of *Romeo and Juliet*, during the following century the view gradually prevailed that Q1 is a stenographic or memorial report; and the theory is now generally accepted that Q1 is a memorial reconstruction of Shakespeare's *Romeo and Juliet*, made by players who were familiar with the promptbook version of Shakespeare's company. (Although there were probably at least two reporters, for convenience they will be here referred to collectively as the Q1 reporter.) Because of gaps in the Q1 text and cuts in the number of necessary players, it has been suggested that Q1 is a memorial report of an abbreviated acting version made by Shakespeare's company from their promptbook.[5] Such a shortened version might well have been prepared for performance in the provinces, and if *Romeo and Juliet* was indeed written by 1592, Shakespeare's company may have performed it there during the period from 1592 to 1594 when the London theaters were closed because of plague. However, it is also possible that many of the lacunae observable in Q1 are memorial errors and that others are cuts stemming from the theatrical use to which the reconstruction itself may have been put, whether in London or the provinces is not clear. The uncertainty is complicated by our ignorance of the purpose for which the text of Q1 was reconstructed. The report may have been made for the specific purpose of providing printer's copy, but since we do not know the price an Elizabethan publisher would pay for a dramatic manuscript, we can only speculate on whether reporting for publication would have been profitable. Or, on the other hand, the report may have been made in order that a group of players without access to a Shakespearian manuscript might give performances of *Romeo and Juliet*, in which case the copy for Q1 may originally have been a promptbook or the foul papers of one. The latter explanation seems perhaps the more probable, but one cannot dogmatize; and difficult as they are, the problems posed by Q1 are only part of the more difficult larger question of Elizabethan bad quartos in general. In any case, Q1, although it was printed two years earlier than Q2, is derived from the promptbook version and therefore represents the text of *Romeo and Juliet* at a later rather than an earlier stage of its history than does Q2.[6] Moreover, the text of Q1, deriving as it does from actual performances, reflects in considerable detail the staging and stage business of a contemporary production in an Elizabethan public playhouse.[7] It is, of course, not the reported Q1 version but rather the promptbook version of Shakespeare's company which is referred to on the title page of Q1, in the statement that *Romeo and Juliet* had been 'often (with great applause) played publicly by the right Honorable the Lord of Hunsdon his Servants,' for the Chamberlain's Men were so styled from July 1596 to April 1597.

The general nature of the variations between Q1 and Q2 can be only briefly illustrated here. The text of Mercutio's death speech, for example, corresponding to III.1.92–112 in Q2 and the present edition, reads in Q1 as follows:

Tybalt under Romeo's arm thrusts Mercutio in, and flies.

Mercutio. Is he gone? hath he nothing? A pox on your houses.
Romeo. What! art thou hurt, man? The wound is not deep.
Mercutio. No, not so deep as a well, not so wide as a barn

door—but it will serve, I warrant. What meant you to come between us? I was hurt under your arm.

Romeo. I did all for the best.

Mercutio. A pox of your houses, I am fairly dress'd. Sirrah, go fetch me a surgeon.

Boy. I go, my lord.

Mercutio. I am pepper'd for this world, I am sped. I' faith, he hath made worms' meat of me. And ye ask for me tomorrow, you shall find me a grave man. A pox of your houses! I shall be fairly mounted upon four men's shoulders— For your house of the Montagues and the Capulets! And then some peasantly rogue, some sexton, some base slave shall write my epitaph— that Tybalt came and broke the Prince's laws, and Mercutio was slain for the first and second cause. Where's the surgeon?

Boy. He's come, sir.

Mercutio. Now he'll keep a mumbling in my guts on the other side. Come Benvolio, lend me thy hand. A pox of your houses!

Exeunt.

Although this passage varies considerably from Q2, one feels that the Q1 reporter here imitated at least the spirit if not the letter of Shakespeare's words; but elsewhere, and as a rule, the reporter grossly mistakes or subtly debases Shakespeare's original text. Two further examples will suffice to illustrate these effects of memorial transmission. One is the substitution in Q1 of the name Francis for Lawrence, obviously suggested by the Friar's invocations of the founder of his order (II.2 SD); and the other is the garbling of 'Mercy but murders, pardoning those that kill,' which appears in Q1 as 'Mercy to all but mud'rers, pardoning none that kill' (III.1.201). Other examples may be culled at random from one of the parallel-text editions.[8]

Q2 and Q1 are both 'substantive' editions in the sense that each was printed from a manuscript, and all other editions are 'derivative' from these two.[9] However, Q2 may be more precisely described as a 'mixed' text,[10] since in the course of printing it suffered 'contamination' by Q1. That is, in addition to Shakespeare's foul papers, an exemplar of Q1 was in part used as copy for Q2, as is evident from sporadic 'bibliographical links' between the two editions.[11] The most striking of these are common typographical peculiarities such as italic print for the Nurse's speeches in I.3 and identical turnovers in prose lineation at I.3.5 and 17. In fact, the 85-line passage from I.2.54 to I.3.36 appears to have been printed directly from Q1 without editorial correction, for, in addition to the bibliographical links between them, the two editions here vary in only four trivial readings. But the contamination is not limited to this passage. In other sections of the text, although Q2 additions and extensive textual variants suggest that the Q2 compositor worked chiefly from Shakespeare's manuscript, bibliographical links occasionally reveal the influence of Q1. Two hypotheses have been suggested in explanation of this contamination. One is that an edited exemplar of Q1 served in part as copy for Q2, and the other is that an unedited exemplar of Q1 was occasionally consulted by the Q2 compositor. The hypothesis of an 'edited quarto' assumes that an editor was given Shakespeare's foul papers, an exemplar of Q1, and the task of preparing copy for Q2. According to a tentatively proposed form of the hypothesis, the editor tore occasional 'good' leaves out of his First Quarto, corrected them with pen and ink so as to bring their text into conformity with that of Shakespeare's manuscript, and interleaved them with manuscript leaves transcribed from that manuscript.[12] Elsewhere the present writer has advanced objections to this hypothesis of 'composite' copy and in its place developed the hypothesis of 'occasional consultation.'[13] This hypothesis, which has been adopted in the present edition, abandons the postulate of an editor. It assumes, rather, that the Q2 compositor was provided with Shakespeare's foul papers and (because of a defect in them) with an uncorrected exemplar of Q1. The compositor set most of his text from the foul papers, but because of a defective or missing leaf in that manuscript he set up the 85-line passage from I.2.54 to I.3.36 directly from Q1. (If we assume that Shakespeare's foul papers contained about fifty lines to a page, or a hundred to a leaf,[14] the passage in question may have been written on the fourth leaf of Shakespeare's manuscript, since the preceding text of the play amounts to about three hundred lines.) Having therefore an exemplar of Q1 at hand, in other parts of the text the Q2 compositor occasionally consulted Q1, either to verify a difficult reading in Shakespeare's foul papers (such as *Rosaline* at II.3.5) or to derive from Q1 a stage direction absent from the foul papers (such as that at II.3.107). Then, wishing to avoid the unnecessary labor of immediately returning to his manuscript copy only to locate the same place he had just found in his quarto copy, the compositor set up directly from Q1 the line or two he could carry in his head; and when, after doing so, he again needed to consult copy, he returned to his chief copy, Shakespeare's foul papers. Thus the Q2 compositor occasionally reproduced, in the text which he was setting mainly from manuscript, certain of Q1's typographical peculiarities and perhaps some of its textual readings.

The first of the early 'derivative' editions was Q3, printed from Q2 in 1609 with a scattering of corrections. It seems likely that the editor was the Q3 compositor since he generally emended only misprints and of Q2's larger errors only corrected one, the omission of a speech heading at II.1.226. Q3 served as copy for the First Folio (1623), where the text was further corrected but carelessly printed.[15] The F1 editor's corrections appear to be conjectural emendations without Shakespearian or playhouse authority. F1 in turn served as copy for F2 (1632), whose editor made 114 deliberate editorial changes in the text, more than in any other play in the First Folio.[16] Again it seems clear that the corrections have no substantive authority. The F2 editor's emendations initiated an editorial tradition which passed more or less unchanged through F3 (1663) and F4 (1685) to Rowe's edition of 1709. None of these editions was contaminated by Q1. On the other hand, the editor of the undated Q4 (printed from Q3 between 1609 and 1637) occasionally consulted Q1 and on its authority vigorously emended the text.[17] Thus he also established an editorial tradition, which passed to Q5 (1637) and to Pope's edition of 1723. Considering that it is a derivative edition, Q4 has had an unusually great influence on the received text through the use made of it by Pope, who, presumably being ignorant of its derivation from Q3, may well have assumed it to be earlier than Q1, with which it agrees in many important particulars to the exclusion of Q2. Pope consulted Q1 as well as Q4, and, since in any case he appears to have considered Q2's variations from Q1 to be spurious changes and additions by the players,[18] he not surprisingly omitted from his edition some sections of the text originating with Q2 and freely introduced to it attractive Q1 variants and the assignment of speeches in Q1 and Q4. An example of Pope's eclecticism is the Q1 variant *name*, traditionally substituted for Q2's *word* in 'a rose By any other word would smell as sweet' (II.1.85–6). This eclecticism was somewhat curbed by Theobald (1733) and succeeding editors, and in the 19th and 20th centuries editors have tended to use fewer and fewer Q1 variants. However, the text was finally purged of such subjective eclecticism only in an edition of 1947,[19] and the present edition is the first to challenge Pope's assignment of a number of speeches. Examples of Pope's considerable influence on the modern editorial tradition are discussed in the notes to II.1. 226–9 and 230–3.

The interrelationship of the various early editions of *Romeo and Juliet* is summarized by the following stemma, in which an asterisk indicates a lost manuscript (hypothetical in the case of the promptbook), a solid line direct transmission, a double line memorial transmission, and a broken line contamination:

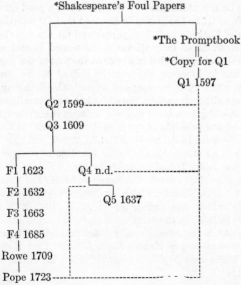

In preparing the present edition, the editor has used Q2 as
copy text. Compositor's errors and corruptions originating with
Shakespeare's foul papers are corrected, silently where obvious
but with a footnote where the change affects the substance of
the reading. Abbreviations are expanded. The designation of
characters is generally normalized in speech headings and stage
directions, and the punctuation and spelling are modernized,
except for occasional forms like *umpeer* which reflect an Elizabethan pronunciation (IV.1.63). The passage from I.2.54 to
I.3.36 is reprinted from Q1, the only substantive source of this
section of the text.[20] Two lines omitted from Q2 are supplied
from Q1 (I.4.7–8). The Q1 stage directions are generally incorporated in the present text, enclosed however in angle brackets
in order to remind the reader that, while most of them probably
indicate the action and stage business of Shakespeare's company,
some of them may have originated with another group of players.
The editor has not hesitated to emend a reading common to the
two substantive editions where Q1 appears to be corrupt and Q2
to have been contaminated by Q1; but where a good Q2 reading
varies from Q1 he has generally assumed that Q2 reproduces the
reading of Shakespeare's foul papers and Q1 the reporter's memorial error. About forty Q1 variants are used, in each case the
debt to Q1 being recorded in a note at the foot of the page. This
eclecticism is, however, deliberately limited to the use of Q1
variants where Q2 is corrupt; and where both editions appear to
be corrupt although variant, the editor has conjecturally emended
the Q2 reading to a third reading, without regard to Q1.[21] Examples of the principle of Q2 emendation without reference to
Q1 are discussed in the notes to II.1.38, 226–9, and 230–3.

There is no external evidence for the date of composition of
Romeo and Juliet. It had undoubtedly been written by 1596, for
the title page of Q1 records that *Romeo and Juliet* had been 'often'
played by Lord Hunsdon's Men—a designation of Shakespeare's
company which was superseded in April 1597. It is usually
assigned to 1595, on the evidence of stylistic resemblances to the
sonnets and to plays traditionally dated between 1594 and 1596:
The Two Gentlemen of Verona, *Love's Labour's Lost*, *Richard II*,
and *A Midsummer Night's Dream*. However, the dating of some

of these works is equally conjectural as that of *Romeo and Juliet*, and the argument of style is inconclusive, since it could also be maintained that parts of *Romeo and Juliet* resemble Shakespeare's earliest work, traditionally dated in the opening years of the 1590's. If in the future Shakespeare's sonnets and first few plays are redated somewhat earlier, more respect may be accorded the date of 1591 which, since there was an earthquake in England in 1580, is suggested by the Nurse's statement that Juliet's weaning is 'since the earthquake now eleven years' (I.3.25). The implication of this topical allusion is usually rejected, in part because *Romeo and Juliet* was a popular play and there are no extant references to it before 1598. However, if the play was written in 1591 or 1592, it might have been performed only a few times before the plague closed London theaters in 1592;[22] and thus its popularity may date from the reopening of theaters in 1594. A conservative conjecture for the date of composition is 1591 or 1592.

NOTES TO APPENDIX A

1. *Romeo and Juliet, Second Quarto, 1599,* London, 1949 (fac. ed.).

2. See R. B. McKerrow, 'A Suggestion Regarding Shakespeare's Manuscripts,' *The Review of English Studies,* 11 (1935), 459–65.

3. The revisional duplications are briefly discussed in the notes to II.1.230–3 and V.3.102; and a full discussion appears in the present writer's article, 'The Corrupting Influence of the Bad Quarto on the Received Text of *Romeo and Juliet,*' *Shakespeare Quarterly,* 4 (1953), 28–32 (hereafter referred to as 'The Received Text').

4. *Romeo and Juliet by William Shakspere, the First Quarto, 1597,* London, 1886 (fac. ed.).

5. H. R. Hoppe, *The Bad Quarto of Romeo and Juliet,* Cornell University Press, 1948.

6. This view, a corollary to the memorial-reconstruction theory, is supported by a comparison of the revisional duplications in Q2 with their corresponding passages in Q1, for in each of the three longer examples it is substantially the revised version which appears in Q1 (II.1.230–3, III.3.40–3, and V.3.108–20). This situation apparently came about because the revisions (rather than the original versions) were incorporated in the promptbook when it was transcribed from the foul papers which later became the copy for Q2; and accordingly the revisions, having been used in the theater, were substantially reproduced in the copy for Q1 by a reporter familiar with performances. The evidence of the revisional duplications thus disproves the theory that Q1 represents an early draft of Q2, for Shakespeare, in writing out the manuscript which later became the copy for Q2, would not in three separate instances have revised a passage in a source-manuscript (which later became the copy for Q1) and then have made of his first revision a second revision in which he returned substantially to the original text of his source.

7. See Richard Hosley, 'The Use of the Upper Stage in *Romeo and Juliet,*' *Shakespeare Quarterly,* 5 (1954).

8. *Romeo and Juliet, Parallel Texts of the First Two Quartos,*

ed. P. A. Daniel, London, 1874, or *Shakespeare's Romeo und Julia*' ed. Tycho Mommsen, Oldenburg, 1859.

9. See R. B. McKerrow, *Prolegomena for the Oxford Shakespeare*, Oxford, 1939, p. 8.

10. See Sir Walter Greg, *The Editorial Problem in Shakespeare*, Oxford, 1942, pp. xiv–xvii.

11. Sidney Thomas, 'The Bibliographical Links Between the First Two Quartos of *Romeo and Juliet*,' *The Review of English Studies*, *25* (1949), 110–14.

12. G. I. Duthie, 'The Text of Shakespeare's *Romeo and Juliet*,' *Studies in Bibliography*, *4* (1952), 3–18.

13. 'The Received Text,' pp. 12–16.

14. See Greg, *The Editorial Problem in Shakespeare*, p. 24.

15. Charlton Hinman, 'The Proof-Reading of the First Folio Text of *Romeo and Juliet*,' *Studies in Bibliography*, *6* (1954), 61–70.

16. M. W. Black and M. A. Shaaber, *Shakespeare's Seventeenth-Century Editors 1632–1685*, New York, 1937, p. 32.

17. *Romeo and Juliet by William Shakspere, the Undated Quarto*, London, 1887 (fac. ed.). Examples of individual Q1 readings which the Q4 editor substituted for those of Q2 and Q3 are *agill* for *aged* (III.1.170), *thou* for *then* (III.3.52), *pronounce* for *prouaunt* (II.1.10), *doue* for *day* (II.1.10), and *open Et cætera* for *open* (II.1.38).

18. *The Works of Shakespeare*, 6 vols., London, 1723–25, *1*, xvi.

19. *The Tragedy of Romeo and Juliet*, ed. H. R. Hoppe, Crofts Classics, New York, 1947.

20. Duthie, 'The Text of Shakespeare's *Romeo and Juliet*,' pp. 22–3.

21. See 'The Received Text,' pp. 20–1.

22. James G. McManaway, 'Recent Studies in Shakespeare's Chronology,' *Shakespeare Survey*, *3* (1950), 25–6.

APPENDIX B

Sources

Although 'separation' and 'potion' romances analogous to *Romeo and Juliet* can be traced back to Ovid and the early Christian Xenophon of Ephesus, the essential features of Shakespeare's plot first appear in the thirty-third story of Masuccio Salernitano's *Novellino*, published at Naples in 1476.[1] In Masuccio, however, there is no mention of rival families, so that the secrecy of the lovers' marriage is unmotivated. Mariotto is banished from Siena for killing a fellow citizen, and by means of a friar's potion Giannozza escapes being forced into a second marriage. After the friar restores her to consciousness, Giannozza follows Mariotto to Alexandria; but in the meanwhile Mariotto, ignorant of her action, has returned to Siena, only to be apprehended and executed. Giannozza retires to a convent where she dies of grief.

Directly or indirectly, Masuccio's story of Mariotto and Giannozza became the source of over a dozen versions of the legend of Romeo and Juliet in half a dozen languages of Renaissance Europe.[2] It is the direct source of Luigi da Porto's *Historia novellamente ritrovata di due nobili amanti, con la lor pietosa morte*, published at Venice around 1530.[3] Here the lovers are first called Romeo and Giulietta, and fiction is first confounded with history by da Porto's associating their families with the historical Montecchi and Cappelletti, mentioned as examples of civil dissension by Dante in the *Purgatorio* (VI. 106). (The Montecchi appear to have been a 13th-century faction in Verona and the Cappelletti a party in Cremona during the same century. The erroneous conception of the two unrelated political groups as opposed Veronese families originates with late 14th-century commentators on Dante.) Since da Porto asserts that the events of his story occurred in Verona during the reign of Bartolommeo della Scala (Shakespeare's Prince Escalus), the legend of Romeo and Juliet came ultimately to be accepted as history. Thus a Renaissance historian of Verona recorded that the lovers died in the year 1303, and the tourist in Verona will still be shown the alleged tomb of Giulietta.

Shakespeare may or may not have read da Porto's novella, but in any case it initiated a tradition which culminates in Shakespeare's direct source. In addition to naming the lovers Romeo and Giulietta and setting them against a background of civil strife, da Porto names the Friar Lorenzo; invents the characters of Marcuccio, Tebaldo, and the Conte di Lodrone (Shakespeare's Mercutio, Tybalt, and Paris); develops the characters of Giulietta's mother and father; introduces the meeting of the lovers at a Cappelletti ball which Romeo attends in disguise; considerably develops the psychology, dialogue, and actions of the lovers beyond Masuccio; and, possibly under the influence of Ovid's story of Pyramus and Thisbe (*Metamorphoses*, IV. 55–166), substitutes for Masuccio's ending substantially Shakespeare's, except that Giulietta's suitor does not appear at the tomb and that Giulietta awakens before Romeo dies of poison and herself commits suicide by holding her breath.

Da Porto's novella is in turn the source of one of Matteo Bandello's *Novelle* (1554), 'La Sfortunata Morte di due infelicissimi amanti, che l'uno di veleno e l'altro di dolore morirono.' [4] Bandello's story is essentially da Porto's, but he adds to the tradition many details which occur in Shakespeare: the name Paris di Lodrone; an unnamed character corresponding to Benvolio; the character of the Nurse, who takes over the plot functions of Giulietta's maid and her servant Pietro in da Porto; the window scene and the rope ladder; and the character of Fra Anselmo (Shakespeare's Friar John) who, being quarantined for plague, fails to inform Romeo of the potion plot. Bandello also makes the Cappelletti the aggressors in the fight in which Romeo kills Tebaldo, and he amplifies the love scenes, probably under the influence of an earlier Italian version by Gerardo Boldieri (1553).

In 1559 Bandello's novella was translated into French with a few significant variations by Pierre Boisteau as the third of his *Histoires Tragiques*, 'L'Histoire de deux amants, dont l'un mourut de venin, l'autre de tristesse.' Boisteau derives the character of the apothecary from an earlier French version by Adrien Sevin (1542), and he changes Bandello's ending by causing Rhomeo to die before Juliette awakens and Juliette to kill herself with Rhomeo's knife. In 1562 Boisteau's *histoire* was adapted into English by Arthur Brooke as a long poem in poulter's measure entitled *The Tragical History of Romeus and Juliet, written first in Italian by Bandell, and now in English by Ar. Br.*[5] This appears to be Shakespeare's immediate and only source. Brooke invents the name of Friar John, adds much description and dialogue, develops the idea of Fortune as arbitress of the lovers' destiny, and introduces the conception of the Nurse as a garrulous old woman. Brooke was probably influenced by a lost play on Romeo and Juliet, for, in his rabidly Protestant preface (where he interprets his theme as filial disobedience), he says that he recently saw 'the same argument' as that of his poem 'set forth on stage' with more commendation than he can look for. This tantalizing reference may be to a French *Roméo et Juliette* which was apparently in existence around 1560. Such a play would probably not, however, have come to Shakespeare's attention; and even if the piece to which Brooke alludes was English, its early date and the absence of evidence that it was ever printed suggest that it probably did not influence Shakespeare, except perhaps indirectly through Brooke's poem. In 1567 Boisteau's version of Bandello was literally translated into English prose by William Painter as the twenty-fifth novel in the second volume of his *Palace of Pleasure*, 'The Goodly History of the True and Constant Love between Rhomeo and Julietta.'[6] Shakespeare had probably read Painter's novella, but he appears not to have made direct use of it. Other versions of the legend, such as a tragi-comedy by Lope de Vega entitled *Los Castelvines y Monteses*, have no bearing on Shakespeare's play.

Shakespeare follows Brooke closely in the details of his plot, but the stage required him to make several shifts of emphasis in structure and character delineation.[7] He unifies the action and gives it a sense of urgency by compressing its duration from months to less than four days, and unlike Brooke and earlier writers he introduces most of his minor characters immediately. Thus the audience is prepared first for Tybalt's death (the cause of the lovers' separation) by his ominous appearances in the opening scene and again at the Capulets' feast, and secondly for the projected marriage with Paris (the cause of Juliet's drinking the potion) by his appearance in the second scene as Juliet's suitor.

The death of Paris at Juliet's tomb is also Shakespeare's innovation. Shakespeare keeps his political theme in the audience's mind from beginning to end by thrice staging the crescendo of a fight followed by entrances of the higher ranks of both houses, a mob of outraged Citizens, and the Prince, symbol of civil authority and order. He gives the Friar a sympathetic character and a homiletic fondness for analogies between the soul of man and the external world of nature. He develops Brooke's portrait of the Nurse by heightening her vulgarity, and he creates the comic character of the pompous but tetchy old Capulet. He invents the name of Benvolio the well-wisher, and from a hint in Brooke he creates the character of Mercutio the realist, forever running atilt at such worshipers of convention as Tybalt the honor-mongering duelist and Rosaline's posturing lover Romeo. In Brooke's poem Mercutio is only briefly characterized (after da Porto's original conception) as

> A courtier that each where was highly had in price,
> For he was courteous of his speech, and pleasant of device.
> Even as a lion would among the lambs be bold,
> Such was among the bashful maids Mercutio to behold.
> With friendly gripe he seized fair Juliet's snowish hand:
> A gift he had that Nature gave him in his swathing band,
> That frozen mountain ice was never half so cold,
> As were his hands, though ne'er so near the fire he did them
>   hold.

(Romeus and Juliet, ll. 255–62)

After this single incident at the Capulets' feast Brooke's Mercutio does not reappear. Shakespeare's Mercutio, however, is almost as central a character as Juliet or Romeo, for his death is the keystone of the plot's structure and his satirical thrusts at Romeo's Petrarchan love and Tybalt's meticulous fencing help to define Shakespeare's chief contributions to the legend, the full-bodied and closely related themes of love and civil disorder. Certainly Shakespeare's play is the tragedy of 'star-cross'd lovers,' but certainly also the members of Shakespeare's audience, endowed with a Tudor abhorrence of civil war, were aware of the Prince's errors of policy in permitting rival factions to exist within the state; and the Prince himself, echoing Machiavelli's condemnation of misguided clemency, belatedly recognizes that 'Mercy but murders, pardoning those that kill' (III.1.201). Thus Shakespeare leavens his love story with a commonplace theme of Renaissance political theory.

NOTES TO APPENDIX B

1. *The Novellino of Masuccio*, tr. W. G. Waters, 2 vols., London, 1895, *2*, 155–65.

2. Olin H. Moore, *The Legend of Romeo and Juliet*, The Ohio State University Press, 1950.

3. 'The recently discovered story of two noble lovers, with their pitiable death,' *The Original Story of Romeo and Juliet by Luigi da Porto*, tr. G. Pace-Sanfelice, Cambridge, 1868.

4. 'The unfortunate death of two most unhappy lovers, one of whom died of poison and the other of grief,' *Novellieri Italiani: Matteo Bandello, Twelve Stories*, tr. Percy Pinkerton, London, 1895, pp. 169–233.

5. *Romeus and Juliet*, ed. P. A. Daniel, London, 1875, or *Brooke's Romeus and Juliet*, ed. J. J. Munro, London, 1908.

6. *Rhomeo and Julietta*, ed. P. A. Daniel, London, 1875.

7. R. A. Law, 'On Shakespeare's Changes of his Source Material in *Romeo and Juliet*,' University of Texas *Studies in English, 9* (1929), 86–102.

APPENDIX C

Reading List

H. B. CHARLTON, *Romeo and Juliet as an Experimental Tragedy*, British Academy Shakespeare Lecture, London, 1939, parts of which are reproduced in the same writer's *Shakespearian Tragedy*, Cambridge University Press, 1949, pp. 49–63 (sources and the Renaissance concept of tragedy).

HARLEY GRANVILLE-BARKER, *Prefaces to Shakespeare*, 2d ser., London, 1930, pp. 1–66, or the Princeton University Press ed., 1947, *2*, 300–49 (structure, staging, and character).

GEORGE LYMAN KITTREDGE, ed., *The Tragedy of Romeo and Juliet*, Ginn & Co., 1940 (full annotation).

G. WILSON KNIGHT, *Principles of Shakespearian Production with Especial Reference to the Tragedies*, London, 1936, pp. 55–7 and 117–25, or the Pelican Books ed., 1949, pp. 39–40 and 84–90 (staging and symbolism).

MOODY E. PRIOR, *The Language of Tragedy*, Columbia University Press, 1947, pp. 61–73 (style and imagery).

E. E. STOLL, *Shakespeare's Young Lovers*, Oxford University Press, 1937, pp. 1–44 (plot and character).